Onboarding Teachers

Onboarding Teachers

A Playbook for Getting New Staff Up to Speed

Nancy Frey

Michelle Shin

Douglas Fisher

Enrico Biscocho

CORWIN
Fisher & Frey

FOR INFORMATION:

Corwin

A SAGE Company

2455 Teller Road

Thousand Oaks, California 91320

(800) 233-9936

www.corwin.com

SAGE Publications Ltd.

1 Oliver's Yard

55 City Road

London EC1Y 1SP

United Kingdom

SAGE Publications India Pvt. Ltd.

Unit No 323-333, Third Floor, F-Block

International Trade Tower Nehru Place

New Delhi 110 019

India

SAGE Publications Asia-Pacific Pte. Ltd.

18 Cross Street #10-10/11/12

China Square Central

Singapore 048423

Vice President and
  Editorial Director: Monica Eckman

Senior Acquisitions Editor: Tanya Ghans

Content Development
  Manager: Desirée A. Bartlett

Senior Editorial Assistant: Nyle De Leon

Production Editor: Melanie Birdsall

Typesetter: C&M Digitals (P) Ltd.

Proofreader: Jeff Bryant

Indexer: Sheila Hill

Cover Designer: Scott Van Atta

Marketing Manager: Morgan Fox

Printed in the United States of America

ISBN 9781071913468

Library of Congress Control Number: 2023939200

This book is printed on acid-free paper.

23 24 25 26 27 10 9 8 7 6 5 4 3 2 1

Contents

Visit the companion website at
https://qrs.ly/9mesfwe
for additional resources.

Acknowledgments

Corwin gratefully acknowledges the contributions of the following reviewers:

Deann Carr, New Teacher Support Manager
Madera, California

Gisela Cruz Hawley, Teacher on Special Assignment
Fresno Unified School District
Fresno, California

Virginia E. Kelsen, Director of Human Resources
El Rancho Unified School District
Claremont, California

Louis Lim, Principal
Bur Oak Secondary School
Toronto, Ontario, Canada

Angela M. Mosley, Professor
Brightpoint Community College
Henrico, Virginia

Tanna Nicely, Principal
South Knoxville Elementary School
Knoxville, Tennessee

Kimberly White, Teacher on Special Assignment
Fresno Unified
Fresno, California

INTRODUCTION

BUILDING A NEW GENERATION OF EDUCATORS

In This Section

- **Onboarding Versus Induction**

- **The Research Base**

- **Using the Playbook**

A Welcoming and Necessary Onboarding Process

It's the start of a new school year, and principal Kendra Watkins and instructional coach David Reese are reviewing plans for welcoming the three new teachers who will be joining their staff this year. And although all three are new to the school, they come from very different backgrounds. Angelina Franklin recently completed Teach for America training and is eager to have her first classroom. Melissa Vasquez taught for a few years but took several years away from the profession to raise a young family. She is now returning to teaching but is new to the state after the recent career transfer of her husband, a member of the military. Jonathan Hill is also new to the profession, having completed his teaching credential program at a local university, and this will be his first assignment. He and Franklin will be enrolled in the district's induction program for first- and second-year teachers. While all three have different support needs, one held in common: onboarding them to a new school organization.

Onboarding should not be confused with orientation. Orientation is typically performed at the district level by the Human Resources office and usually includes employment and insurance requirements and logistics. These are essential for new hires, but the orientation does not provide new teachers with information about the context of their daily teaching.

Onboarding should not be confused with induction. New teachers are required to complete professional learning experiences, known as an induction program, to develop their newly acquired skills. If we think back to our induction program, we certainly grew from our collaboration with new educators, but it did not fully prepare us for what we needed to know at the site level.

What Is Onboarding?

Onboarding is the employment process of integrating a new professional member into the site-level organization. Coherent onboarding processes have several characteristics: (1) planned activities aligned to the site's values and structures; (2) regular opportunities to network with other members of the organization, including those who perform similar job functions; and (3) extended experiences that last up to one year.

Each campus is unique, with its own set of curricular, instructional, and cultural expectations, hence the need for a robust onboarding process. As an example, it is likely that Angelina, who has not gone through an extended teacher preparation program, and Jonathan, who has recently finished one, are likely to be additionally enrolled in a district or state induction program. Melissa, a credentialed teacher who is returning to the profession after several years away, will not be involved in a formal induction program. But as school site leaders, newly hired teachers like Angelina, Melissa, and Jonathan can all benefit from coherent support and guidance about the school's ways of work.

An excellent onboarding process should provide new employees, regardless of experience, with guidance about how the site-level organization functions, why it does so, and what success looks like. Gallup, which specializes in analytics and advisory for other companies, has offices in dozens of countries around the world. They recognized the complexity of onboarding at their sites and developed their own to integrate employees new to their offices. They advise that an effective onboarding process should help new members answer these five questions (Gallup, 2019, p. 12):

The Five Questions of Onboarding

1. What do we believe in around here?
2. What are my strengths?
3. What is my role?
4. Who are my partners?
5. What does my future here look like?

The onboarding process is developed at the site by instructional leaders and coaches. They begin by customizing what is broadly taught in teacher preparation programs. Then they articulate their localized expectations and coach new staff members so they can equitably contribute and serve students, their families, and the collective school community. Additionally, and arguably just as important, is the welcoming and collaborative spirit of onboarding. Protheroe (2006) found that teachers who are new to school organizations, regardless of experience:

▸ Want access to accessible leaders who provide assistance, guidance, and solutions

▸ Appreciate being observed in the classroom and getting direct feedback and guidance

▸ Want to be listened to and made to feel successful

▸ Benefit from a support group of teachers with whom they can collaborate, vent, and provide motivation during tough times

▸ Are eager to watch experts and develop their craft under guidance

▸ Want more information about the expectations of school leaders

As Gallup notes in their onboarding process, failed, laissez-faire onboarding moves new hires from "excitement to disillusionment . . . 'This isn't what I expected. Maybe there's a better place for me.'" (p. 12). On the other hand, a successful onboard process moves those new to the organization from "excitement to long-term commitment . . . 'This is better than I expected. I think I have a future here!'" (p. 12).

Principal Watkins and instructional coach Reese have a plan in mind to support each of these teachers during their first year at school, with the intended outcome of gaining long-term commitment. Using the monthly plan outlined in this playbook, they coordinate their efforts to ensure that each of these new teachers—Angelina, Jonathan, and Melissa—is successful. This playbook offers instructional leaders, coaches, and mentors the tools to provide teachers new to your site with these valuable opportunities.

The Research Base

This playbook draws from two bodies of research: supports for novice teachers in their first year, as well as those who may be returning to the profession after an extended time away, and the Visible Learning® database.

District, regional, and university induction programs are of value in continuing the professional learning of early-career teachers. However, most have little direct influence on site-based supports that new teachers need to cultivate their craft and build their self-efficacy. School site leaders have the unique ability to shape the collegial networks that exist in their schools, which is of vital importance in the lives of new teachers (Frahm & Cianca, 2021). The importance of a teacher's sense of efficacy, which is to say their belief that they can act upon their individual goals, cannot be minimized. The efficacy of the teacher has been linked to student learning and job satisfaction, crucial for teacher retention in the first five years (Klassen & Chiu, 2010).

Hylton and Colley (2022) in their review of findings of a new teacher support initiative, offered four recommendations that we believe resonate for site leaders, coaches, and mentors who support new teachers in their buildings:

> **Novice teachers have a lot on their minds.** Being a new teacher is a bit like drinking out of a fire hose—there are so many stimuli coming all at once that it can be nearly impossible to sort out what is notable versus what is just noise. Site leaders, coaches, and mentors help novice teachers notice what is informative and act upon it. They prioritize, but they also help new teachers to filter.

> **Novice teachers are hungry for meaningful engagement.** Daily teaching can come as a shock to new teachers, especially those who experience it as a largely isolating experience. Not only do they need adult contact, but they also crave guidance from leaders that includes regular feedback. Most of all, they need lots of opportunities to see colleagues in action and to hold discussions where they can pose questions.

> **Novice teachers need safe spaces to explore and even fail.** Reflective teaching requires that we pay close attention to what is working and what is not and respond accordingly. But new teachers may hold a naïve belief that they need to somehow be "perfect." Having a safe space to explore means that they have permission to take measured and informed risks, and to notice its impact. Without guidance, novice teachers can either fall into a pattern of blaming students or blaming themselves, with little insight into finding a path forward.

> **We *all* keep learning.** Perhaps this is the most exciting finding that Hylton and Colley (2022) reported: The benefits to leaders, coaches, mentors, and novice teachers in mutual. As a field, we often speak of the

new learning that novice teachers can bring to the building, but unless we are deliberate in building linkages between seasoned and new staff, the opportunity is never realized. Communication with new teachers makes these benefits possible.

The second research base we draw from is Visible Learning, which describes a constellation of efforts. It is a research database (www.visiblelearningmetax.com; Visible Learning Meta[X], 2021), a school improvement initiative (see Corwin, n.d., https://us.corwin.com/en-us/nam/visible-learning), and a call to action to focus on what works best to impact learning (Hattie, 2023). The Visible Learning database is composed of over 2,100 meta-analyses of the work of over 400 million students. That is big data when it comes to education. In fact, some have said that it is the largest educational research database amassed to date. To make sense of so much data, John Hattie focuses his work on interpreting the meaning of these meta-analyses.

A meta-analysis is a statistical tool for combining findings from different studies with the goal of identifying patterns that can inform practice. In other words, it is a study of studies. The tool that is used to aggregate the information is an effect size. An effect size is the magnitude, or size, of a given effect. To draw an imperfect but functional comparison, consider what you know about how earthquakes are measured. They are reported as an order of magnitude on a scale called a Richter scale. Some earthquakes are imperceptible except by specialized measurement tools. Other earthquakes have a minimal shake that results in a small, momentary impact but no lasting effects. A few register high on the Richter scale and have a definitive impact on an area. Just as numbers on the Richter scale help us understand the effect of an earthquake, effect sizes from meta-analyses of several studies help us understand the impact of an educational influence. Understanding the effect size lets us know how powerful a given influence is in changing achievement—in other words, the impact of the effort.

John was able to demonstrate that influences, strategies, actions, and so on with an effect size greater than 0.40 allow students to learn at an appropriate rate, meaning at least a year of growth for a year in school. While it provides an overall average, often specific conditions can be more critical—such as whether you are measuring a narrow construct (like vocabulary words known) or a wider construct (such as creative thinking). Throughout this playbook, certain practices are supported with descriptions of their effect sizes. In doing so, we want to support your efforts in guiding novice teachers with research-backed findings. The Meta[X] website at www.visblelearningmetax.com provides further information about the particular influences mentioned.

Who Is This Playbook for?

The support of teachers new to the site cannot be left to chance, yet too often, it happens anyway. The repercussions of what occurs when support is left to chance are profound and long lasting. Eleven percent (11%) of novice teachers leave the profession within the first year (Zhang et al., 2019). Nearly half will leave before their fifth year (Burke et al., 2015). And keep in mind that these were pre-pandemic findings. In an era where teacher recruitment and retention are crucial for the profession, we must develop more coherent webs of support that ensure we don't lose early-career educators. Relying on an induction program is not enough. And here's a bit more encouragement if you're not quite sold on the idea of creating a coherent onboarding process for those who are new to your site: "Employees who describe their onboarding process as exceptional are 3.3 times more likely to strongly agree that their job is as good, or better, than expected" (Gallup, 2019, p. 7). Importantly, these are the product of human interactions that together create a relational network for new teachers. A comprehensive web of site-based new teacher supports includes the following:

- Central office induction leaders
- School administrators
- Department and grade-level chairs
- Instructional coaches
- Mentor teachers who are welcoming a new colleague into their department or grade level
- Expert teachers who care about the future of the profession

Is this you? If so, this playbook is for you. You'll find ideas for how to support teachers new at their school sites, systematically and intentionally, during their first year of teaching.

Using This Playbook

The playbook is designed for instructional leaders, coaches, mentors, and expert teachers to design and implement an effective onboarding process for new staff. We will use the term *new teachers* to include novice teachers who are new to the profession as well as more experienced professionals who have been away from teaching for several years and are now returning. There are eight cycles based on focused themes specific to the needs of a first-year teacher:

Cycle 1: Setting up the physical environment, routines, and procedures

Cycle 2: Invitational teaching, student engagement, and universal classroom management

Cycle 3: Teacher credibility, high-expectations teaching, and family communication

Cycle 4: Teacher clarity

Cycle 5: Fostering student ownership of learning and using evidence-based instructional practices

Cycle 6: Monitoring progress through formative assessment and feedback

Cycle 7: Mastery of standards and grading

Cycle 8: Closing the school year and moving forward

Each cycle has several interactive features, designed for you individually (the instructional leader, coach, or mentor), for you to do with the new teacher, and for the new teacher to experience on their own. Each cycle begins with a Context About the Theme section that serves as a brief summary of the current research on the topic. We believe that leaders, coaches, mentors, and expert teachers will find these summaries useful in deepening their own expertise. In addition, features include coaching scenarios, coaching reflections, checklists for implementation, self-assessments, applications to practice, review of the previous learning, as well as learning walk, observation, and debriefing tools. In addition, we have short reviews written for you to ground the cycle's theme in the context of current research.

The cycles are intended to be presented in sequential order but can be used as standalone topics. Similarly, although each one is designed for four-week cycles, some themes may understandably go beyond that timeline. You'll find specific coaching questions aligned to the cycle, and activities designed to help the novice teacher return to previous themes as they acquire new learning and experiences. Each onboarding process is unique, so we encourage you to modify the learning such that it aligns with your district or schoolwide focus and meets the needs of your new teachers.

We fully recognize that these topics are not one-and-done; they cannot be fully covered in the span of four weeks. Rather, we hope that this incremental approach provides you with opportunities to spotlight district and site initiatives, while also establishing the evergreen nature of these topics. They remain relevant throughout one's teaching career.

Leaders are the second greatest influence on student learning, and teachers have the greatest impact. Equity-driven leaders make it a priority to coach all teachers because of their undeniable impact on students, but they also differentiate their support and develop a welcoming learning environment for the new adult learners on their staff. Our hope is that this playbook will serve as a guide, but we also hope that it reminds you of why you became an educator in the first place. We play an incredibly important and undeniable role in mentoring the next generation of equity-driven teachers.

CYCLE 1
PLANNING FOR YOUR FIRST DAY OF SCHOOL

In This Section

- Setting Up the Physical Environment

- Routines

- Procedures

Context About the Theme of Planning for Your First Day of School

There are few things more exciting to new teachers than getting the key to set up the physical environment of their classroom. The fall buzz can be felt on campus as everyone prepares for students' first week back to school. Even seasoned teachers report back from the summer eager to get back to their classrooms. When a new group of students enters their learning space for the first time, what impression do we want to make? We want teachers, especially new ones, to be intentional in leaving a positive and long-lasting one. In other words, we make choices that are deliberate, calculated, intended, purposeful, and planned. Make the most of the set-up time before students arrive by focusing their attention on the decisions they make about the physical environment, and about the routines and procedures they will put into place.

New teachers begin to make a positive first impression through thoughtful choices about the way they set up their physical classroom. Posters, plastic organizers, and colorful bins are great but they are not required nor do they guarantee an intentionally inviting classroom. We've seen too many classrooms that seem more social media–friendly than student-friendly. The space should reflect the functionality of the young people who are in it. In addition, the environment should be print-rich such that it promotes the literacies used to learn. Finally, the spaces should be organized, tidy, and orderly; one does not have to spend hundreds of dollars for students to know that you care about the space that you all share.

The routines and procedures taught by the teacher need to align with the physical and desired psychological environment. These routines and procedures should answer the question, "How do we learn and work together?" Since this is the teacher's first year, they may have trouble imagining potential and realistic scenarios on their own. Instructional leaders and coaches can support them directly by sharing their own experiences with students. They have an opportunity to explain why thinking ahead and being prepared with protocols minimizes unwanted distractions. Thus begins an important dialogue about setting a foundation for effective classroom management.

In Their Shoes

Establishing Your Classroom Environment Leader Reflection

Directions: Instructional leaders, coaches, and mentors are not only effective because they bring a wealth of knowledge and experience to their role but also because they connect with their coachees' reality and recall how they felt when they were in the same position.

Since it may have been a few years since you were a first-year teacher, let's take a step back to remember and put ourselves in their shoes.

1. Describe the physical environment of your first-year classroom.

_____

_____

_____

_____

_____

2. Were there rookie mistakes you made in your set-up? If so, what were they and how did you correct them?

_____

_____

_____

_____

_____

3. As a new educator, what was challenging about creating routines and procedures that worked for you and your students?

_____

_____

_____

_____

_____

4. How did you turn your area(s) of growth into an area(s) of strength?

_____

_____

_____

_____

_____

(Continued)

(Continued)

5. Looking back, what coaching support did you receive? What do you wish you would have received?

_____

_____

_____

_____

_____

6. How will you incorporate your own experience when developing your instructional coaching plan for your new teachers? How will you meet the needs of new teachers?

_____

_____

_____

_____

_____

Coaching for Reflection

In each cycle, we will offer a scenario to practice preparing for a coaching conversation. Coaching is not about identifying what is wrong, but rather what is next. This requires asking questions that mediate the thinking of the coachee. Costa and Garmston's (2015) work on cognitive coaching focuses exactly on this approach. We have gathered questions from several sources to use in your coaching practice (see Figure 1.1). We keep a list of these questions in our notebooks so that when coaching opportunities arise, we are ready.

Figure 1.1   Coaching Questions to Support Meaningful Learning

Nine Coaching Questions to Mediate Thinking (School Reform Initiative, 2023)

1. Why do you think this is the case?
2. What do you feel is right?
3. What is your hunch about . . . ?

4. What was your intention when . . . ?

5. What surprises you about . . . ? Why are you surprised?

6. What is the best thing that could happen?

7. What are you most afraid will happen?

8. What do you need to ask to better understand?

9. What is the one thing you won't compromise?

Four Questions for Coachable Actions for Planning (Student Understanding)

1. How will you know what misconceptions your students possess?

2. How will you know what they understand?

3. What evidence will you accept for this understanding?

4. How will you use their understanding to plan future instruction?

Four Cognitive Coaching Questions for Planning (Teacher Insights) (Costa & Garmston, 2015)

1. What is a near-term goal that you have for your students or for yourself?

2. What might success look like or sound like?

3. What are some strategies that you have used before that might be successful with this group? What are your hunches?

4. What is most important for you to pay attention to in yourself?

A Question to Ask After the Lesson (Costa & Garmston, 2015)

In what ways was the lesson you *planned* different from the lesson you *taught*?

Supportive Relational Conditions (Costa & Garmston, 2015)

1. Pausing

2. Paraphrasing

3. Posing questions

4. Providing data

5. Putting ideas on the table

6. Paying attention to self and others

7. Presuming positive intention

When a Teacher Is Stuck (Paraphrasing)

You're feeling [label the emotion] because [name the content of their concern] and what you're looking for is [goal] and you're looking for a way to make that happen [pathway].

Coaching Scenario for Leaders

Principal Nissa

Directions: Read the scenario below and consider what you would do if you were in Principal Nissa's position. Then answer the follow-up questions below.

Today is the teachers' first day back to work from summer break. Milo is a brand new, first-year teacher. As he enters his classroom for the first time, he quickly realizes that there will be a lot of work to prepare a space that will be inviting and productive for his students. In his credential classes, he saw multiple examples of inviting classrooms, spaces for collaboration, and colorful photo-ready classes.

Principal Nissa walks to every classroom to personally welcome each teacher back. When she enters Milo's room, she sees that he is deep in thought and looking distraught. He shares that he wants to transform his blank canvas and has been on the computer, shopping for decor, posters, and supplies. He worries that he isn't able to buy everything he wants to create an intentionally inviting space.

Follow-Up Questions

1. If you were Principal Nissa, what recommendations would you give to Milo for creating an inviting physical space for all students? Consider the walls, screen, orientation, tables, posters, boards, and walkways.

_____

_____

_____

_____

_____

2. Where are some resources to get classroom supplies (e.g., furniture, shelves, tables, chairs)? Consider the district warehouse, other classrooms, other teachers, and retiring teachers.

_____

_____

_____

_____

_____

3. What recommendations or guidance would you share with Milo so he doesn't feel pressured to spend his own money to furnish his classroom?

_____

_____

_____

_____

_____

Coaching Scenario for Leaders

Nima

Directions: Read the scenario below and consider what you would do if you were Nima's mentor or coach. Then answer the follow-up questions below.

Nima is new to the school and shares that she wants to work on two short-term goals before school starts: (1) a good physical classroom arrangement, and (2) effective routines. She is passionate about these two areas because she is committed to developing a safe learning environment with positive relationships with and among her students. Nima asks you to help her think through her next steps.

Follow-Up Questions

1. What are the top three things that new teachers need to know about routines and procedures?

_____

_____

_____

_____

_____

(Continued)

(Continued)

2. Nima is a new teacher so she may not anticipate the need for some routines or procedures. What scenarios will you prepare beforehand to share with her? How will they help her in being proactive, not reactive?

_____

_____

_____

_____

3. What coaching questions will you ask to facilitate Nima's thinking and next steps around classroom routines and procedures?

_____

_____

_____

_____

4. What resources or professional development might you share with Nima? What additional coaching support would you offer?

_____

_____

_____

_____

Leaders Get Clear and Anticipate

With a strong onboarding process, instructional leaders and coaches send a clear message to new teachers about best practices. They communicate and reiterate the site's expectations around student and family engagement. This minimizes ambiguity so new teachers adapt and adopt best practices more quickly than if they were to navigate this on their own.

In Our Shoes

Conveying the Culture and Climate of the School Leader Reflection

Directions: Instructional leaders, coaches, and mentors should pause first to get clear about their expectations. Then they can craft their message and provide onboarded teachers with appropriate feedback to elevate their practice.

1. Do teachers have a clear understanding of the goals of the school's culture and climate? If so, what are the agreed-upon expectations?

_____

_____

_____

_____

2. How does the organization help new teachers develop and maintain these values and practices?

_____

_____

_____

_____

3. What factors can hinder a new teacher's ability to create these experiences?

_____

_____

_____

_____

(Continued)

(Continued)

4   How do you address and support them through their challenges?

_____

_____

_____

_____

_____

5. What unique challenges do you anticipate new teachers will encounter?

_____

_____

_____

_____

_____

6. What key routines are already in place schoolwide? This may include restroom procedures, movement through the building, sending students on errands, and dismissal routines.

_____

_____

_____

_____

7. Misunderstandings about the cell phone policy at the site are likely to derail new teachers and those returning to the profession. What is the cell phone policy for students at your school? What is the cell phone policy for adults at your school? How are these explained to students, families, and teachers?

_____

_____

_____

_____

_____

Leaders Get Clear and Communicate

Now that you have a clear vision of this month's focus and what that looks like at your site, it is important to communicate this message along with your expectations. Below you will find a sample of an onboarding checklist with a suggested timeline for three groups of deliverables: Leader/Coach, New Teacher, and Together.

Onboarding Checklist

	LEADER/COACH	NEW TEACHER	TOGETHER
Planning Week	Send a reminder email to new teachers about the upcoming monthly onboarding check-in meeting.	Complete the New Teachers Get Familiar and Implement interactions.	
	Put a note of appreciation in new teachers' office mailboxes. A handwritten note addressed to the new teacher will light up their day!		
	Complete the Context About the Theme section, including the interactions.		
	Complete the Leaders Get Clear and Anticipate section, including the interactions.		
	Review the Cycle 1 learning guide and slide deck at the companion website and make modifications as needed.		
	Invite expert teachers to join the onboarding meeting and share their best practices with new teachers. Ask them if they would welcome new teachers to visit their classrooms and ask for their availability.		
	Facilitate the monthly onboarding check-in meeting. This meeting is short (up to 30 minutes), and might occur before school, at lunch, or after school. We have provided a slide presentation for you to use and customize. Bring water and healthy snacks as tokens of appreciation.	Schedule time to visit an expert teacher's room. Complete the pre-work on the New Teachers Learn From Expert Teachers interactive feature.	Attend the monthly onboarding check-in meeting.

(Continued)

(Continued)

	LEADER/COACH	NEW TEACHER	TOGETHER
	Schedule a ghost learning walk. Include expert teacher classrooms in the list of classrooms to visit.	Visit the expert teacher's classroom. Use the New Teachers Learn From Expert Teachers interactive feature to document your learning. Thank the expert teacher in person or by email for inviting you into their classroom.	Attend the ghost learning walk.
	Send a thank-you email to new teachers for attending the onboarding meeting. Confirm the dates for observation and post-observation meetings via calendar invites. Send a thank-you email to the expert teachers who attended the onboarding meeting and invite new teachers to visit their classrooms.		
	Review the New Teachers Get Familiar and Implement section, including the interactions.		
	Give them an end-of-the-month token of appreciation to congratulate them on successfully entering the school year.	Complete the Ghost Walk interaction.	
	Review responses from the Ghost Walk interactions.		
	Complete the Trust Recalibration interaction.		
	Send a reminder email about next month's onboarding meeting (date, time, location). Include calendar invites.		

Email to New Teachers on the First Day of Cycle

(Example)

Hello _____,

Welcome to the new school year—we are so thrilled to have you on our campus and are so happy that you chose to be a part of our team!

As we begin this month, I want to personally invite you to our first onboarding meeting on _____. I invited all new teachers and expert teachers to join us so we can build community and share experiences and best practices. This week, we will discuss how to effectively set up your physical classroom, routines, and procedures.

I am looking forward to supporting and getting to know you this year. It's going to be great!

Sincerely,

_____

(Other Conversations to Consider)

- District and schoolwide committee meetings
- District and schoolwide professional development opportunities
- Local and community events
- Staff socials and events
- Student events:
  - Theater performances
  - Chorus concerts
  - Band and orchestra concerts
  - Dance competitions
  - Athletic events, games, tournaments
  - School fundraisers
  - School dances

Invitational Email to Expert Teachers

(Example)

Hello _____,

Welcome to the new school year—I hope you had a wonderful, much-needed break.

This year, we have _____ new teachers who joined our team. My goal is to work closely with them throughout the year and to support their transition through an onboarding process. For the next several weeks, I will share our site's expectations on _____ and offer resources and ongoing support in this area. I have attached a summary of this cycle's theme [attach the Context About the Theme found at the beginning of this cycle].

Our new teachers want to see best practices in action and would benefit so much from hearing about what you do, how you do it, lessons learned, and any other words of wisdom you are willing to share. Since you are an experienced and expert teacher in this area, I want to invite you to help me mentor our new staff. Would you be willing to open your classroom doors for new teachers and those new to our school to learn from you?

Our first onboarding meeting is on _____. I invited all new teachers and expert teachers to join us so we can build community and share experiences and best practices. I hope you will say yes and join us.

Thank you for shaping the next generation of educators!

Sincerely,

_____

Leaders Express Appreciation

Here is a checklist of ways that leaders/coaches can show a token of their appreciation to new teachers for all of their hard work. This could also show your teachers how to pay it forward. Showing them graciousness will move them to show and connect with their students. We recommend that you do one item from this checklist this month to make them feel welcome and a part of the school.

(Examples)

Write a one- or two-sentence message on a thank-you card. Put it in their office mailbox with a special treat:

[School or district swag]

- Lanyards
- T-shirts or sweaters from student council or ASB
- Accessories like scarves, hats, socks, etc.
- Pencils, mugs, tumblers, etc. with the school or district logo

Expert Tip: Check if there are forgotten items from previous years in the site or district supply rooms.

[Items they may need in their classrooms]

- Tissue
- Pencils or pens
- Paper
- Wipes
- Whiteboard markers
- Smelly markers
- Composition notebooks
- Gift baskets of supplies

Expert Tip: Ask parent/family groups, community members, or local businesses for donations.

[Other gift ideas]

- Gently used novels
- Reusable shopping bags or canvas tote bags
- Boxed thank-you cards

New Teachers Get Familiar and Implement

Video Reflection

Welcome to My Classroom

Directions: After watching Video 1.1 (available at the companion website), answer each of the questions below.

1. What qualities and conditions do you believe contribute to her welcoming environment?

_____

_____

_____

_____

_____

(Continued)

(Continued)

2. How does this teacher integrate her physical environment with routines and procedures?

_____

_____

_____

_____

_____

3. List three ways the classroom environment is organized, orderly, and tidy.

_____

_____

_____

_____

_____

4. What additional routines and procedures do you need to put in place to maintain an organized, orderly, and tidy environment?

_____

_____

_____

_____

_____

New Teachers Self-Assess

A Welcoming Classroom

Directions: Take a moment to tap into your prior knowledge and assess your learning space.

1. On a scale of 1 to 5 (with 1 being least inviting and 5 being most inviting), rate how welcoming your classroom is. Explain your reasoning.

_____

_____

_____

_____

2. Think back to when you were a student. What impact did the classroom environment have on you as a learner?

_____

_____

_____

_____

3. In what ways are your classroom's physical features intentionally inclusive and accessible? Be specific.

_____

_____

_____

_____

4. Scan your room. Are there any aspects that students could identify as unintentionally exclusive (e.g., signs that say, "No students allowed")?

_____

_____

_____

_____

New Teachers Self-Assess

Routines and Procedures

Directions: Take a moment to tap into your prior knowledge and assess your areas of strength and growth in this area.

1. On a scale of 1 to 5 (with 1 being low and 5 being high), how organized are you in your personal or professional life? Explain.

    _____

    _____

    _____

    _____

    _____

2. What routines and procedures do you personally use? How do they help you to manage time and space?

    _____

    _____

    _____

    _____

    _____

3. Think back to when you were a student. What impact did having (or not having) classroom routines and procedures have on you as a learner? On the learning environment? Be specific.

    _____

    _____

    _____

    _____

    _____

Your Turn

Set Up a Welcoming Classroom

Directions: We shared common understanding and expectations around how to set up our physical environments, routines, and procedures. Answer each prompt below to reflect and determine next steps.

1. How will you set up your physical classroom so that students feel welcome and know that you care about the space they are in?

_____

_____

_____

_____

_____

2. Reflect on the routines and procedures that are currently in place. Do you need to adjust or make modifications before students' first day?

_____

_____

_____

_____

_____

3. Are there classroom structures that you didn't consider before? What procedures do you need to develop before students arrive?

_____

_____

_____

_____

_____

Check-In and Follow-Up Tools for Leaders

Each of us knows the significance of a first impression. From firsthand experience, we know that it can be long lasting and not easy to change, for better or for worse. The reality is that our students, families, and even colleagues see our classrooms as an extension of who we are. It is not unreasonable to think that they make assumptions about our professional competency based on what they see. Having an intentionally inviting and welcoming space matters.

The Ghost Walk is a type of learning walk that instructional leaders and coaches, accompanied by new teachers, can use either before students' first day back or within the first month of school. Teachers open their classrooms without students present, and guests observe the physical learning environments. The entire visit takes about 30 minutes to one hour and time is set aside at the end to collectively process the evidence and wonderings.

An effective onboarding process invites new teachers to see each other's newly designed classrooms and visit expert teachers' rooms as well. This experience opens their eyes to different possibilities and gives them an opportunity to collaborate and develop their professional growth.

Classroom Notetaking Tool

Ghost Walk

	EVIDENCE	NOTES	WONDERINGS
Classroom A (New Teacher)			
Classroom B (New Teacher)			
Classroom C (New Teacher)			

	EVIDENCE	NOTES	WONDERINGS
Classroom D (Expert Teacher)			
Classroom E (Expert Teacher)			
Classroom F (Expert Teacher)			

Post-Learning Walk Debrief

Ghost Walk

	CLASSROOMS A, B, AND C	CLASSROOMS D, E, AND F
Emerging Patterns and Trends		

(Continued)

(Continued)

	CLASSROOMS A, B, AND C	CLASSROOMS D, E, AND F
What inviting features did you notice?		
What routines and procedures did you notice?		
What will you do differently as a result of this experience?		
In what ways was this process helpful or not helpful? **How can I better support you?**		

Source: Adapted from Fisher et al. (2019, pp. 90–94).

New Teachers Learn From Expert Teachers

Physical Classroom, Routines, and Procedures

Directions: You have an amazing opportunity to collaborate with and visit an expert teacher on your site. This tool is designed to ensure that you have a learning experience that will directly impact your practice with your students.

Pre-Visit Preparation

Before visiting the classroom, what are three questions that you want to ask the expert teacher related to the themes? Capture their responses below.

QUESTIONS	ANSWERS

Look-Fors During the Visit

What three elements are you looking for or hoping to see? Document evidence of those look-fors below.

LOOK-FORS (PHYSICAL ENVIRONMENT, ROUTINES, AND PROCEDURES)	EVIDENCE

(Continued)

(Continued)

Post-Visit Reflection

Reflect on the visit to the expert teacher's classroom. Answer each question below.

1. How will this visit support your growth as a new and effective teacher?

2. What specific strategies or tools will you take back to your classroom?

3. Do you have any follow-up questions that you would like to ask the expert teacher?

Expert Tip: Send the expert teacher a thank-you email and include what you enjoyed about their classroom and how visiting them made you a better teacher!

Leaders Ask "How Did We Do?"

Setting Up the Physical Environment, Routines, and Procedures

It is very important for me to gauge my effectiveness as a coach because I want to provide a welcoming work environment and make you feel appreciated—because you are! Please help me in meeting these goals.

Using the following scale, with 1 being not confident, 3 being somewhat confident, and 5 indicating very confident, how confident are you in your ability to do the following as it relates to the physical environment, and establishing routines and procedures?

Thank you for all that you do!

"I know where I'm going."

I understand my current performance and how it relates to my professional growth.

1 · · · · · · 2 · · · · · · 3 · · · · · · 4 · · · · · · 5

Please elaborate:

"I have the tools for the journey."

I understand that I can select from a range of strategies to move my learning forward, especially when progress is interrupted.

1 · · · · · · 2 · · · · · · 3 · · · · · · 4 · · · · · · 5

Please elaborate:

"I monitor my progress."

I seek and respond to feedback from others to assess my own performance. I know that making mistakes is expected and indicates an opportunity for further learning.

1 · · · · · · 2 · · · · · · 3 · · · · · · 4 · · · · · · 5

Please elaborate:

"I recognize when I'm ready for what's next."

I make my own observations to identify when I'm ready to move on.

1 · · · · · · 2 · · · · · · 3 · · · · · · 4 · · · · · · 5

Please elaborate:

"I know what to do next."

I know what to do when I don't know what to do. I know how to research, organize information, and continue my own learning.

1 · · · · · · 2 · · · · · · 3 · · · · · · 4 · · · · · · 5

Please elaborate:

What further questions and support needs do you have for me?

Tying It Together With Trust

The trustworthiness of school leaders by faculty directly impacts the achievement of their students (Tschannen-Moran & Gareis, 2015). Trustworthy leaders demonstrate behaviors within the five facets of trust intentionally and with consistency. These five facets of trustworthiness in leaders include (Tschannen-Moran, 2004):

> **Benevolence:** This is the most essential facet of trust and refers to a perceived sense of caring on the part of others. The leader is perceived as having their best interests at heart and believes the leader can protect them from harm.

> **Reliability:** The sense that the leader will consistently come through for them when needed.

> **Competence:** The belief that the leader has the skills to protect the core of school—teaching and learning—and manage the school effectively.

> **Honesty:** The sense that the leader's character and integrity are truthful and consistent with their words and actions.

> **Openness:** Demonstrated through the sharing of information, control, and influence. Others are allowed to initiate and provide input about plans, goals, and resources.

Consider taking a moment to pause and reflect on your behaviors and interactions with your staff at this crucial start of the school year:

> In what ways did you develop trust specifically with new teachers?

> Were there any instances in which you unintentionally acted in a way that might have resulted in lowering their trust?

> As we move into the next month, what will you continue doing? What will you start doing? What will you stop doing?

Trust Recalibration

Looking Back to Move Forward

	EVIDENCE OF TRUSTING BEHAVIORS	EVIDENCE OF DISTRUSTING BEHAVIORS	HOW WILL I MAINTAIN OR DEVELOP TRUST NEXT MONTH?
(1) Benevolence			
(2) Reliability			
(3) Competence			
(4) Honesty			
(5) Openness			

Conclusion

Principals, instructional coaches, mentors, and expert teachers work with new teachers and those new to the site to create a welcoming classroom. In this cycle, we focused on setting up the physical classroom, routines, and procedures. It is important to have these ready before students arrive to prevent potential unwanted distractions to the learning environment. It sets a tone for positive outcomes in student learning and well-being not only for the first month but throughout the year.

Additional Resources

For Leaders and Coaches

Sweeney, D., Harris, L. S., & Steele, J. (2022). *Moves for launching a new year of student-centered coaching.* Corwin.

A 5-Minute Read for New Teachers

Pariser, S. (2018, September 6). Prep where it counts before the start of school. *Corwin Connect.* https://corwin-connect.com/2018/09/prep-where-it-counts-before-the-start-of-school/

An 8-Minute Read for Expert Teachers

Gonsor, S. (2022, July 29). The qualities of exceptional mentor teachers. *Edutopia.* https://www.edutopia.org/article/qualities-exceptional-mentor-teachers/

Visit the companion website at
https://qrs.ly/9mesfwe
for additional resources.

CYCLE 2
STARTING OUT STRONG
(4 WEEKS)

In This Section

- Intentionally Inviting Teachers

- Introduction to Student Engagement

- Universal Classroom Management

Context About the Theme of Starting Out Strong

The first day of school is a magical one. Students fill the hallways and they greet each other, excited to reunite with friends whom they have not seen since the last day of school. Teachers wrap up their final preparations with interruptions from students who stop to say hi, while some sit down and chat about what they did during their time off. In either case, whether they want to admit it or not, they missed being in school because they missed their peers and also because they missed their teachers. Teachers have the greatest impact on student learning, and it is through the ongoing trusting relationships they develop with students that allow learning to thrive. In this cycle, we will focus on three areas that can assist new teachers in experiencing early success:

 ▶ Invitational Teaching

 ▶ An Introduction to Student Engagement

 ▶ Classroom Management

Because of the interdependent relationships between these dimensions, it is useful for novice teachers to see that they are not mutually exclusive.

Invitational Teaching

Purkey and Novak (1996) describe invitational education through four psychological elements: *trust, respect, optimism*, and *intentionality*. When teachers and students trust each other, they assume positive intentions and have shared responsibility and investment to build, maintain, and repair their relationships. The second lens is respect, which is a result of actions that communicate mutual understanding of another's autonomy, identity, and value to the community. Optimism is a hopeful assumption that the potential of each classroom member is untapped, and every member of the classroom (this includes the teacher and all students) is responsible for finding ways to help others reach their potential. The fourth construct, intentionality, means that classrooms and schools carefully design their practices, policies, processes, and programs to convey trust, respect, and optimism.

These same researchers extended the ideas of intentionality and invitational education and identified four types of teachers (see Figure 2.1). We'll discuss each quadrant beginning at the top left and moving counter-clockwise. An *intentionally uninviting teacher* is rare and we wonder why they chose to work in schools at all. They are hurtful and leave an incredibly negative impact on students' learning and well-being. *Unintentionally uninviting teachers* exhibit deficit thinking, have low expectations for students, and hold pessimistic beliefs about school improvement efforts. They are not conscious of the fact that their low expectations are felt loud and clear by students. *Unintentionally inviting teachers* reach many students because of their enthusiasm but have limits to their craft. They don't reflect on their professional practice, so they have a surface-level approach to instruction. Lastly, *intentionally inviting teachers* hone their craft with purpose and precision. They use self-reflection and an asset-based lens to ensure that they reach all students.

Figure 2.1   Four Types of Teachers

INTENTIONALLY UNINVITING TEACHERS . . .	INTENTIONALLY INVITING TEACHERS . . .
• Are judgmental and belittling • Display little care or regard • Are uninterested in the lives and feelings of students • Isolate themselves from school life • Seek power over students	• Are consistent and steady with students • Notice learning and struggle • Respond regularly with feedback • Seek to build, maintain, and repair relationships
UNINTENTIONALLY UNINVITING TEACHERS . . .	**UNINTENTIONALLY INVITING TEACHERS . . .**
• Distance themselves from students • Have low expectations • Don't feel effective and blame students for shortcomings • Fail to notice student learning or struggle • Offer little feedback to learners	• Are eager but unreflective • Are energetic but rigid when facing problems • Are unaware of what works in their practice and why • Have fewer means for responding when student learning is resistant to their usual methods

Source: Fisher, Frey, Quaglia, et al. (2018, p. 8). Based on the work of Purkey and Novak (1996).

Novice teachers often start out as being unintentionally inviting. Their enthusiasm is captivating, but they possess less ability to reflect on their teaching and are less resilient when confronted with challenges. In fact, we wonder if those intentionally disinviting teachers started out their careers as enthusiastic but unreflective novice teachers who got hurt and hardened their hearts.

Student Engagement

Great teachers understand how to engage their students. Student engagement is the dynamic relationship between three components: the teacher, the student, and the content (see Figure 2.2). Teachers optimize learning when they form positive relationships with their students, communicate what they will learn via learning intentions, and how they demonstrate that they have learned it with success criteria. (We will return to the topic of teacher clarity in more depth during Cycle 4. For now, we want to plant the seed that when students know what is expected of them, it reduces anxiety, disengagement, and problematic behavior.) They also present the content through challenging and worthwhile tasks, which motivate students to engage. As educators, we aim to hit the sweet spot as often as possible—when the three dimensions overlap and intersect.

Figure 2.2 Model of Engagement by Design

Source: Fisher, Frey, Quaglia, et al. (2018, p. 13).

Some educators, especially those who are new to the profession, misunderstand engagement and use words that describe compliant student behavior. Behavioral engagement is easy to observe and it can easily mislead an observer into believing that a student's outward actions automatically mirror their interior lives. Effective teachers shift their attention between cognitive and emotional engagement because it allows them to more accurately gauge student learning. They look beyond outward behavior and listen to the discussion. They inquire directly with students about their interaction with the content. In other words, they are more interested in what students are thinking than in how they are acting.

Universal Classroom Management

Say the phrase "classroom management" to most novice teachers and you'll find that many define it in terms of discipline. To be sure, school discipline protocols are an essential element of running a classroom. Every novice teacher should be fully debriefed about the protocols used when there is a significant student disruption. But the major portion of a classroom management plan is proactive. As discussed in Cycle 1, it includes routines and procedures so that students and the teacher are on the same page about how work gets done.

Beyond that, novice teachers should design for universal classroom management, or evidence-based, proactive approaches designed to reduce problematic behavior while promoting a positive classroom climate (Martin et al., 2016):

  ▶ **Teacher self-regulation:** Understanding how one's own emotions influence student behavior and your responses

  ▶ **Constructing an image of caring and authority:** High authority is balanced by an even high degree of compassion; a "warm demander" expects much and is supportive of those efforts (Vasquez, 1989)

- **Opportunities for response:** Frequent response opportunities, including universal and choral responses and peer discussions, promote learning and engagement and reduce disruption

- **Intentional relationship building:** Not only with the students who immediately warm to you but also with those hard-to-reach, hard-to-teach students; as one teacher said, "Find a way to make your hardest kid your favorite kid"

- **Classroom community:** Actions and traditions that build and reinforce an *esprit de corps*

- **Developmentally and culturally responsive**: The language or learning is developmentally consistent and draws on the assets and unique abilities of the young people they teach

Classroom management can facilitate or hinder student engagement; new teachers would be remiss not to be thoughtful about this plan. It includes strategies that minimize the potential for disruptions and describe how teachers will respond when they happen. Instructional leaders, coaches, and mentors know that the key to an effective classroom management plan is its primary focus on proactive, not the reactive disciplinary action plan that follows after the fact.

In Their Shoes

An Invitational Teacher Leader Reflection

Directions: Instructional leaders, coaches, and mentors are not only effective because they bring a wealth of knowledge and experience to their role but also because they connect with their coachees' reality and recall how they felt when they were in the same position.

Since it may have been a few years since you were a first-year teacher, let's take a step back to remember and put ourselves in their shoes.

1. As you reflect on your first year, which of the four types of teachers were you? Did it change?

_____

_____

_____

_____

_____

(Continued)

(Continued)

2. What strategies did you use in the classroom with your students to build engagement?

_____

_____

_____

_____

_____

3. What challenges did you experience in classroom management as a new educator?

_____

_____

_____

_____

_____

4. What do you know now, as an experienced educator, that you wish you knew back then, as a new teacher?

_____

_____

_____

_____

_____

5. Looking back, what coaching support did you receive? What do you wish you would have received?

_____

_____

_____

_____

_____

6. How will you incorporate your experience when developing your instructional coaching plan? How will you meet the needs of new teachers?

_____

_____

_____

_____

_____

Coaching Scenario for Leaders

Kalina

Directions: Read the scenario below and consider what you would do if you were Kalina's principal, coach, or mentor. Then answer the follow-up questions below.

Kalina shared with you that it's only been two weeks, but she is already struggling with her fourth-period class. She is a teacher who has been away from the profession for six years, and she says that "the kids have changed so much." She discusses student misbehavior and disruptions and admits that her other periods are "okay, I guess" but that fourth period is leaving her emotionally exhausted. She wonders if things would be better with schedule changes for some of the students. Before exploring that route, what do you want to know?

Follow-Up Questions

1. As Kalina's coach, what initial questions might you ask to get a better understanding of the situation?

_____

_____

_____

_____

_____

(Continued)

(Continued)

2. What should Kalina know about supports available in the school?

_____

_____

_____

_____

_____

3. What questions do you want to ask about how she engages students?

_____

_____

_____

_____

_____

4. What questions do you want to ask about her classroom management?

_____

_____

_____

_____

_____

Leaders Get Clear and Anticipate

With a strong onboarding process, instructional leaders and coaches send a clear message to new teachers about "how we do things." They communicate and reiterate the site's expectations around student engagement. This minimizes ambiguity so new teachers adapt and adopt best practices more quickly than if they were to navigate this theme on their own.

In Our Shoes

Student Engagement Leader Reflection

Directions: Instructional leaders, coaches, and mentors should pause first to get clear about their expectations. Then they can craft their message and provide onboarded teachers with appropriate feedback to elevate their practice.

1. What are the shared expectations around student engagement? What are examples and non-examples in the classroom?

_____

_____

_____

_____

_____

2. What professional learning opportunities has the site had around student engagement?

_____

_____

_____

_____

_____

3. What are the top three things that new teachers need to know when it comes to student engagement?

_____

_____

_____

_____

_____

(Continued)

(Continued)

4. What unique challenges do you anticipate new teachers will encounter in engagement and classroom management?

_____

_____

_____

_____

_____

5. How will you differentiate your expectations and support in these areas for new teachers?

_____

_____

_____

_____

_____

In Our Shoes

Universal Classroom Management Leader Reflection

Directions: Instructional leaders, coaches, and mentors should pause first to get clear about their expectations. Then they can craft their message and provide onboarded teachers with appropriate feedback to elevate their practice.

1. What are the site's expectations for all staff regarding universal classroom management?

_____

_____

_____

_____

_____

2. What procedures and systems are used for minor infractions? What is the role of the teacher?

_____

_____

_____

_____

_____

3. What procedures and systems are used for major infractions? What is the role of the teacher?

_____

_____

_____

_____

_____

4. What unique challenges do you anticipate new teachers will encounter? How will you address and support them?

_____

_____

_____

_____

_____

Leaders Get Clear and Communicate

Now that you have a clear vision of this cycle's focus and what that looks like at your site, it is important to communicate this message along with your expectations. On the next page you will find a sample of an onboarding checklist with a suggested timeline for three groups of deliverables: Leader/Coach, New Teacher, and Together.

Onboarding Checklist

	LEADER/COACH	NEW TEACHER	TOGETHER
Week 1	Send a reminder email to new teachers about the upcoming monthly onboarding check-in meeting.	Complete the New Teachers Get Familiar and Implement interactions.	
	Put a note of appreciation in new teachers' office mailboxes. A handwritten note addressed to the new teacher will light up their day!		
	Complete the Context About the Theme section, including the interactions.		
	Complete the Leaders Get Clear and Anticipate section, including the interactions.		
	Review the Cycle 2 learning guide and slide deck at the companion website and make modifications as needed.		
	Invite expert teachers to join the onboarding meeting and share their best practices with new teachers. Ask them if they would welcome new teachers to visit their classrooms and ask for their availability.		
	Facilitate the monthly onboarding check-in meeting. This meeting is short (up to 30 minutes), and might occur before school, at lunch, or after school. We have provided a slide presentation for you to use and customize. Bring water and healthy snacks as tokens of appreciation.	Schedule time to visit an expert teacher's room. Complete the pre-work on the New Teachers Learn From Expert Teachers interactive feature.	Attend the monthly onboarding check-in meeting.
		Visit the expert teacher's classroom. Use the New Teachers Learn From Expert Teachers interactive feature to document your learning. Thank the expert teacher in person or by email for inviting you into their classroom.	Schedule classroom observation focused on the theme. Agree on a data collection tool. Schedule post-observation meeting.

	LEADER/COACH	NEW TEACHER	TOGETHER
Week 2	Send a thank-you email to new teachers for attending the onboarding meeting. Confirm the dates for observation and post-observation meetings via calendar invites. Send a thank-you email to the expert teachers who attended the onboarding meeting and invite new teachers to visit their classrooms.		Conduct classroom observation. Hold the post-observation meeting with a debrief tool.
Week 3	Review the New Teachers Get Familiar and Implement section, including interactions.		
Week 4	Give them an end-of-the-month token of appreciation to congratulate them on successfully completing another month.	Complete the Check-In and Follow-Up tools for interactions.	
	Review and reflect on responses from submitted Leaders Ask "How Did We Do?" surveys.		
	Complete the Trust Recalibration interaction.		
	Send a reminder email about next month's onboarding meeting (date, time, location). Include calendar invites.		

Email to New Teachers on the First Day of Cycle

(Example)

Hello _____,

Congratulations on successfully completing the first week of your first year—I never had any doubts!

As we begin the next chapter of our learning, I want to personally invite you to our next onboarding meeting on _____ to begin our work with student engagement and universal classroom management. I value our time to come together to grow professionally and also as individuals outside of the classroom.

(Continued)

(Continued)

I invited expert teachers to share their insights and open their classroom doors. I'm hopeful that you will find time to take advantage of this opportunity to learn from our best.

We know how hard you are working, so thank you for your commitment. Your success is our success!

Sincerely,

_____

(Other Conversations to Consider)

- District and schoolwide committee meetings
- District and schoolwide professional development opportunities
- Local and community events
- Staff socials and events
- Student events:
  - Theater performances
  - Chorus concerts
  - Band and orchestra concerts
  - Dance competitions
  - Athletic events, games, tournaments
  - School fundraisers
  - School dances

Invitational Email to Expert Teachers

(Example)

Hello _____,

I hope you had a great first week back—I know that the students missed seeing you this summer.

As you know, we have _____ new teachers who joined our team. My goal is to work closely with them throughout the year and to support their transition through an onboarding process. For the next several weeks, we will be focused on invitational teaching, student engagement, and universal classroom management. I have attached a summary of this cycle's theme [attach the Context About the Theme found at the beginning of this cycle]. I will offer resources and ongoing support, but they also asked for my help in identifying expert teachers in these areas.

Our next onboarding meeting is on _____. Our new teachers want to see best practices in action and would benefit so much from hearing about what you do, how you do it, lessons learned, and any other words of wisdom you are willing to share. I immediately thought of you so I want to invite you to help me mentor our new staff. Would you be willing to open your classroom doors so new teachers can learn from you?

I hope you will come join us so we can build community and share experiences and best practices.

Thank you for shaping the next generation of educators!

Sincerely,

_____

Leaders Express Appreciation

Here is a checklist of ways that leaders/coaches can show a token of their appreciation to new teachers for all of their hard work. This could also show your teachers how to pay it forward. Showing them graciousness will move them to show and connect with their students. We recommend that you do one item from this checklist this month to make them feel welcome and a part of the school.

(Examples)

Write a one- or two-sentence message on a thank-you card. Put it in their office mailbox with a special treat:

[School or district swag]

- Lanyards
- T-shirts or sweaters from student council or ASB
- Accessories like scarves, hats, socks, etc.
- Pencils, mugs, tumblers, etc. with the school or district logo

Expert Tip: Check if there are forgotten items from previous years in the site or district supply rooms.

[Items they may need in their classrooms]

- Tissue
- Pencils or pens
- Paper
- Wipes

(Continued)

(Continued)

- Whiteboard markers
- Smelly markers
- Composition notebooks
- Gift baskets of supplies

Expert Tip: Ask parent/family groups, community members, or local businesses for donations.

[Other gift ideas]

- Gently used novels
- Reusable shopping bags or canvas tote bags
- Boxed thank-you cards

New Teachers Get Familiar and Implement

Video Reflection

Be an Intentionally Inviting Teacher

Directions: After watching Video 2.1 (available at the companion website), answer each question below.

1. How does Nancy describe an intentionally inviting teacher?

_____

_____

_____

_____

_____

2. What specific welcoming strategies do the students and teachers highlight in the video?

_____

_____

_____

_____

_____

3. Which strategy resonated most with you?

_____

_____

_____

_____

_____

New Teachers Self-Assess

Be an Intentionally Inviting Teacher

Directions: Take a moment to tap into your prior knowledge and assess yourself in this area of invitational education.

1. Think back to when you were a student. Identify the characteristics of each of the four types of teachers below and reflect on why you put them where they are (no names, please).

_____

_____

_____

_____

_____

INTENTIONALLY UNINVITING TEACHER	INTENTIONALLY INVITING TEACHER
UNINTENTIONALLY UNINVITING TEACHER	UNINTENTIONALLY INVITING TEACHER

(Continued)

(Continued)

2. Which of the four types of teachers do you self-identify as (1) intentionally inviting, (2) intentionally uninviting, (3) unintentionally uninviting, or (4) unintentionally inviting? Why?

_____

_____

_____

_____

_____

3. Which one of the four types of teachers would your students say that you are? Does their answer match yours? Why or why not?

_____

_____

_____

_____

_____

Your Turn

Practice Invitational Teaching

Directions: Now that we have a shared understanding of what invitational teaching is and its four dimensions, it is time to put it to practice with your students. How do you plan to manifest each dimension in tangible and intangible ways?

	OBSERVABLE OUTCOMES
Trust The ongoing relationships between teachers and students	

	OBSERVABLE OUTCOMES
Respect Actions communicate a context where everyone is valued	
Optimism Every member of the classroom has potential every day	
Intentionality Everything is carefully designed to convey trust, respect, and optimism	

Video Reflection

Student Engagement

Directions: Watch Video 2.2 (available at the companion website) and then answer each question below.

1. What are the three components of engagement? What is the significance of the overlapping areas?

   _____

   _____

   _____

   _____

   _____

(Continued)

(Continued)

2. Which type of engagement do educators tend to focus on the most? Why?

_____

_____

_____

_____

_____

3. Which type of engagement should educators focus on more? Why?

_____

_____

_____

_____

_____

New Teachers Self-Assess

Student Engagement

Directions: Take a moment to tap into your prior knowledge and assess yourself in the area of student engagement.

1. What is student engagement? Why does it matter?

_____

_____

_____

_____

2. How do you know when students are engaged? Provide examples that reflect cognitive engagement, not just behavioral.

_____

_____

_____

_____

_____

3. How do you know when students are disengaged? Provide examples.

_____

_____

_____

_____

_____

4. When you are excelling at student engagement, what conditions are present? What are you doing and why? What are you noticing about your own emotional engagement with them?

_____

_____

_____

_____

_____

New Teachers Self-Assess

Universal Classroom Management

Directions: Take a moment to tap into your prior knowledge and assess yourself in principles of universal classroom management (teacher self-regulation, constructing an image of authority and caring, opportunities for response, intentional relationship building, classroom community, and developmentally and culturally responsive).

(Continued)

(Continued)

1. Effective classroom management strategies are built around an 80/20 model, where 80% is proactive and 20% is reactive. In the past week, what was your percentage breakdown?

_____

_____

_____

_____

_____

2. On a scale of 1 to 5 (with 1 being least effective and 5 being most effective), how effective are you in your universal classroom management during this first month of school?

_____

_____

_____

_____

_____

3. What do you need to strengthen?

_____

_____

_____

_____

_____

4. Think back to when you were a student. Now identify a teacher who had effective classroom management. What impact did they have on student engagement and learning outcomes? How were they invitational in their teaching?

_____

_____

_____

_____

_____

5. Have you identified hard-to-reach students in your classes? How have you strived to build relationships with them?

_____

_____

_____

_____

_____

Instructional coaches will discover that many new teachers need their support when it comes to universal classroom management principles. This work requires nothing less than a supportive, nurturing, and committed coach to support them manage conflict and their emotional reactions in a healthy way. We included two effective strategies that all new and experienced teachers should incorporate into their practice.

Your Turn

Practice the 2 × 10 Technique

New teachers can use the 2 × 10 technique to develop strong relationships with students (Wlodkowski, 1983). Spend 2 minutes per day, for 10 consecutive days, interacting with a hard-to-reach student. These conversations do not need to be confined to the classroom. You can strike up conversations with them in the hallway, the lunchroom, and at pick-up and drop-off areas at school. The conversation can be about anything other than school.

Directions: Think about three students who would benefit from your extra support. Then make a plan to initiate and get started!

WHICH STUDENTS WILL YOU FOCUS ON?	WHEN WILL YOU CONNECT WITH THEM?	WHAT NON-SCHOOL-RELATED QUESTIONS WILL YOU ASK?

Your Turn

Practice Affective Statements

Affective statements are "I statements" that elicit reflective thinking. When teachers use them to redirect students, they shift the power structure and minimize negative reactions and maximize neutral emotions. Teachers and students are encouraged to use affective statements to articulate their feelings without being confrontational or escalating the situation.

Directions: Describe three times that you redirected students or had to manage/resolve a conflict this month. Create example statements to address each scenario using the provided sentence starters.

SCENARIO	NON-EXAMPLE STATEMENTS	SENTENCE STARTERS	EXAMPLE STATEMENTS
Phone use during class	"Put away your phone now. Learning should be your priority."	• I am so sorry that . . . • I am concerned that . . . • I am feeling frustrated about/by/to see/to hear . . .	
Tardiness	"There is no excuse for you to be late to class all the time."	• I am having a hard time understanding . . . • I am so pleased by/to see/to hear . . . • I am uncomfortable when I see/hear . . .	
		• I am uneasy about . . . • I am concerned about . . . • I am so thankful that/for . . .	

SCENARIO	NON-EXAMPLE STATEMENTS	SENTENCE STARTERS	EXAMPLE STATEMENTS

Source: Smith et al. (2022, pp. 76–77).

Check-In and Follow-Up Tools for Leaders

Effective school leaders, coaches, and mentors understand that instructional leadership positively impacts learning experiences for students and staff. They model best practices and work side-by-side with new and experienced teachers to support their professional growth. They fill their schedules with classroom observations to see and engage firsthand in teaching and learning processes. This check-in tool is not a formal observation. Rather, it is intended as a brief (10 to 15 minutes), pre-arranged visit to the new teacher's classroom to monitor learning and development related to the development of a welcoming and rigorous learning environment.

Classroom Observation Tool

Invitational Teaching, Student Engagement,
and Universal Classroom Management

DESCRIBE THE ENGAGEMENT BETWEEN THE *TEACHER* AND *STUDENTS*. (RELATIONSHIP)	DID THE *TEACHER* ARTICULATE THE *CONTENT'S* LEARNING INTENTIONS AND SUCCESS CRITERIA? RECORD STUDENT RESPONSES BELOW. (CLARITY)	ARE *STUDENTS* ENGAGED WITH THE *CONTENT* THROUGH WORTHWHILE, CHALLENGING TASKS? (CHALLENGE)
	"What are you learning today?"	
	"Why are you learning it?"	

DESCRIBE THE ENGAGEMENT BETWEEN THE *TEACHER* AND *STUDENTS*. (RELATIONSHIP)	DID THE *TEACHER* ARTICULATE THE *CONTENT'S* LEARNING INTENTIONS AND SUCCESS CRITERIA? RECORD STUDENT RESPONSES BELOW. (CLARITY)	ARE *STUDENTS* ENGAGED WITH THE *CONTENT* THROUGH WORTHWHILE, CHALLENGING TASKS? (CHALLENGE)
	"How will you know you have learned it?"	

Post-Observation Debrief

Invitational Teaching, Student Engagement, and Universal Classroom Management

	RELATIONSHIP	CLARITY	CHALLENGE
Emerging Patterns and Trends			

(Continued)

(Continued)

	RELATIONSHIP	CLARITY	CHALLENGE
What went well? What were your emotions at the time?			
In reflecting back, what would you have done differently? Why?			
What is a near-term goal you have for yourself?			
What is a near-term goal you have for your students?			
How can I support you in meeting your goals for yourself and for your students?			

New teachers are eager to collaborate with colleagues, and effective onboarding processes offer them regular opportunities to do this. One of the ways that they can develop professionally is by working with expert teachers and visiting their classrooms. Instructional leaders and coaches play a pivotal role in connecting them to mentor teachers who add to their collegial network.

New Teachers Learn From Expert Teachers

Student Engagement and Universal Classroom Management

Directions: You have an amazing opportunity to collaborate with and visit an expert teacher on your site. This tool is designed to ensure that you have a learning experience that will directly impact your practice with your students.

Pre-Visit Preparation

Before visiting the classroom, what are three questions that you want to ask the expert teacher related to invitational teaching, student engagement, and/or universal classroom management? Capture their responses below.

QUESTIONS	ANSWERS

Look-Fors During the Visit

What three elements are you looking for or hoping to see? Document evidence of those look-fors below.

LOOK-FORS (INVITATIONAL TEACHING, STUDENT ENGAGEMENT, AND UNIVERSAL CLASSROOM MANAGEMENT)	EVIDENCE

(Continued)

(Continued)

Post-Visit Reflection

Reflect on the visit to the expert teacher's classroom. Answer each question below.

1. How will this visit support your growth as a new and effective teacher?

2. What specific strategies or tools will you take back to your classroom?

3. Do you have any follow-up questions that you would like to ask the expert teacher?

Expert Tip: Send the expert teacher a thank-you email and include what you enjoyed about their classroom and how visiting them made you a better teacher!

Leaders Cycle Back With New Teachers

Thank you for your tireless commitment to our students! As we move forward through our progressions, it is important to revisit what we learned previously so we don't forget and continue to grow in those areas.

Directions: Reflect on our last theme and answer the questions below.

Previous Theme(s)

*   Setting up the physical classroom, routines, and procedures

1. What new takeaways or aha moments did you encounter?

2. In what ways have you developed professionally in this area?

3. What lingering questions or wonderings do you have for a leader, coach, or expert teacher?

Leaders Ask "How Did We Do?"

Invitational Teaching, Student Engagement, and Universal Classroom Management

It is very important for me to gauge my effectiveness as a coach because I want to provide a welcoming work environment and make you feel appreciated—because you are! Please help me in meeting these goals.

Using the following scale, with 1 being not confident, 3 being somewhat confident, and 5 indicating very confident, how confident are you in your ability to do the following as it relates to invitational teaching, student engagement, and universal classroom management?

Thank you for all that you do!

"I know where I'm going." I understand my current performance and how it relates to my professional growth.	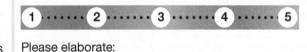 Please elaborate:
"I have the tools for the journey." I understand that I can select from a range of strategies to move my learning forward, especially when progress is interrupted.	 Please elaborate:
"I monitor my progress." I seek and respond to feedback from others to assess my own performance. I know that making mistakes is expected and indicates an opportunity for further learning.	 Please elaborate:

(Continued)

(Continued)

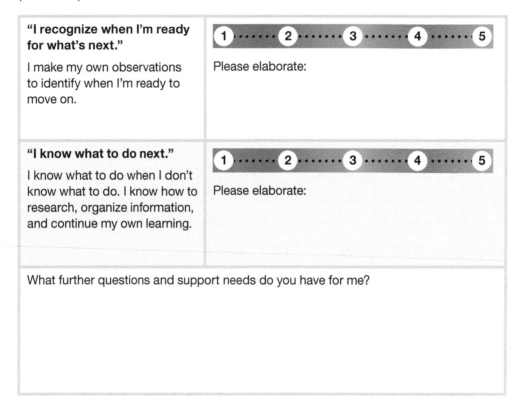

"I recognize when I'm ready for what's next." I make my own observations to identify when I'm ready to move on.	1 ···· 2 ···· 3 ···· 4 ···· 5 Please elaborate:
"I know what to do next." I know what to do when I don't know what to do. I know how to research, organize information, and continue my own learning.	1 ···· 2 ···· 3 ···· 4 ···· 5 Please elaborate:

What further questions and support needs do you have for me?

Tying It Together With Trust

Recall the five facets of trustworthiness in leaders (benevolence, reliability, competence, honesty, and openness) from page 34. Consider taking a moment to pause and reflect on your behaviors and interactions with your staff at the beginning of the school year:

 ▸ In what ways did you develop trust specifically with new teachers?

 ▸ Were there any instances in which you unintentionally acted in a way that might have resulted in lowering their trust?

 ▸ As we move into the next month, what will you continue doing? What will you start doing? What will you stop doing?

Trust Recalibration

Looking Back to Move Forward

	EVIDENCE OF TRUSTING BEHAVIORS	EVIDENCE OF DISTRUSTING BEHAVIORS	HOW WILL I MAINTAIN OR DEVELOP TRUST NEXT MONTH?
(1) Benevolence			
(2) Reliability			
(3) Competence			
(4) Honesty			
(5) Openness			

Conclusion

If new teachers want to increase student engagement, then they also need to think about the principles of universal classroom management and adopt an intentionally inviting teaching style. These dimensions of teaching go a long way in reducing problems that might otherwise arise. However, they aren't a guarantee. New teachers mistakenly believe that conflict is avoidable if they have the perfect lesson plan, but expert teachers know better. It is not a matter of if, but when and how to respond when low-level conflicts or disengagement occur. When intentionally inviting teachers redirect their students, they do it without causing harm to the student and their relationship. In turn, students are less likely to be defensive or confrontational. It is not easy for any teacher, not even an experienced one, to "reset" ineffective classroom management strategies once the school year begins. Putting in the time early in the school year is a worthwhile investment.

Additional Resources

For Leaders and Coaches

Fisher, D., Frey, N., Quaglia, R. J., Smith, D., & Lande, L. L. (2018). *Engagement by design: Creating learning environments where students thrive.* Corwin.

A 6-Minute Read for New Teachers

Gordon, B. (2018, March 23). A five-word answer to student engagement. *Corwin Connect.* https://corwin-connect.com/2018/03/the-five-word-answer-to-student-engagement/

A 5-Minute Read for Expert Teachers

Weinberg, A. (2021, July 19). 3 strategies for productive teacher mentoring. *Edutopia.* https://www.edutopia.org/article/3-strategies-productive-teacher-mentoring/

Visit the companion website at
https://qrs.ly/9mesfwe
for additional resources.

CYCLE 3

HOW ARE WE BUILDING STUDENTS' PERCEPTIONS OF EXCELLENCE?

(4 WEEKS)

In This Section

- **Teacher Credibility (Trust, Competence, Dynamism, and Immediacy)**

- **High-Expectations Teaching**

- **Communicating With Families**

Context About the Theme of Student Perceptions of Excellence

This cycle's theme expands on invitational teaching by going deeper with teacher credibility. While invitational education is a summation of the teaching acts we utilize, teacher credibility speaks to how these acts are perceived by students. Closely related are the ways in which high-expectations teaching is manifested, beyond vague statements that "all students can learn" (we certainly hope so!). The third dimension of student perceptions of excellence is how, and to the extent, we engage with their families. Families are a chief motivator for students. Ten years' worth of student voice data, gathered from more than 450,000 students in grades 6–12, are illuminating. More than 95% of students said that their parents cared about their education (Quaglia Institute, 2019). Yet too often families only hear from the teacher or the school when a problem arises. New teachers need to understand that they have a powerful and positive lever to use—family involvement in their child's education.

Teacher Credibility

A positive student-teacher relationship goes beyond whether students "like" their teachers. Likability feels good, but teacher credibility is what matters. When students believe that their teacher is credible, not only do they believe that they can learn from them, but with an effect size of 0.90, they actually do (Visible Learning Meta[X], 2021). They are also more likely to act in accordance with shared norms and agreements in the class. However, it is dynamic in nature; we believe that "teacher credibility is *always* in play" (Fisher et al., 2016, p. 10).

The challenge is this: We don't get to decide whether we are credible. Our students do so. It is their perception of the teacher's credibility that matters. It makes sense for new teachers to question how much control they have over someone else's perceptions. In other words, can teachers really influence student beliefs? Fortunately, the answer is yes: teacher credibility rests upon trustworthiness, competence, dynamism, and immediacy (see Figure 3.1).

Figure 3.1   Four Elements of Teacher Credibility

TRUSTWORTHY TEACHERS . . .	COMPETENT TEACHERS . . .	DYNAMIC TEACHERS . . .	TEACHERS WITH IMMEDIACY . . .
Care about students as individuals	Are experts in their content	Are passionate	Are accessible and relatable
Know who their students are in and out of the classroom	Deliver their content accurately and coherently	Communicate enthusiasm about the subject and students	Easy to interact with
Have students' best academic and social interests at heart	Organize and pace their lessons appropriately	Capture students' interests	Notice and respond to student verbal and nonverbal signals
Reliable and true to their word (or can explain why they could not keep it)			Do not waste time because learning matters
			Convey urgency without causing undue stress

High-Expectations Teaching

Students *will* meet the expectations that we set for them. Expert teachers set high expectations and their learners successfully rise to the occasion time and time again. The sad reality is that the opposite is also true: with low-expectations teaching, students will meet that bar, too.

Teacher expectations have an effect size of 0.43, meaning that what is expected is closely aligned with what is achieved (Visible Learning Meta[X], 2021). Instructional leaders, coaches, and mentors disrupt and reset false narratives that lead to low-expectations teaching. Expectations are shaped by their attitudes and beliefs about students based on race, ethnicity, and socioeconomic status (Murdock-Perriera & Sedlacek, 2018). A diverse student body adds immeasurable assets that strengthen the school community. There is no place on campus for deficit thinking; it causes harm to individuals and the collective.

The instructional moves of the teacher telegraph their expectations to their students. At the class level, teachers with low expectations (Rubie-Davies, 2014)

- Spend more time reminding students of procedures

- Focus on task completion, not learning

- Ask more closed questions

- Manage behavior negatively and reactively

- Provide little room for student choice

- Link achievement to ability

- Use ability grouping in the classroom

- Provide advanced learning only to high-ability learners, with lots of repetitive, low-level tasks for others

The results of low-expectations teaching are devastating. In one study, students of similar abilities were followed for a year. Their self-described expectations for themselves were parallel at the beginning of the school year. But some had high-expectations teachers, while others were taught by those with low expectations. At the end of the year, those in the high-expectations group significantly outperformed peers in low-expectations classrooms, despite beginning from a similar starting point (Rubie-Davies, 2007).

How are high expectations enacted in daily teaching? Education Hub summarized Rubie-Davies's work, which can easily be used as a series of questions to pose to new teachers:

- Do you regularly ask open questions?

- Do you rephrase questions when answers are not correct?

- Do you check for understanding frequently throughout the lesson to inform feedback?

- Do you provide a range of learning experiences so that students can exercise choice? (trust in learners)

> Do you provide a clear framework for learning? (learning intentions and success criteria)

> Do you set individual goals with learners?

Family Communication

One underutilized means of support are the families of the children they are teaching. We're not talking about volunteering in the classroom. While those are appreciated, most families don't have the time available to do so. In addition to work-hour limitations, families may have language differences or are uncomfortable in a school environment, all of which can serve as barriers to outdated notions of school-based family communication pathways (Epstein et al., 2019). Rather, it is working in partnership with families on a shared goal: the learning and success of their child. This is home-based family engagement and has been demonstrated as effective in promoting positive student behavior and learning in school (Fantuzzo et al., 2004).

School communications with families can be broadly clustered into two forms: those that are informative, and those that are negative (Hine, 2022). Informative communications include

> A child's progress between school reports

> How to help with homework

> Class placement

> Caregiver's expected roles

> College and vocational school news

Hine's analysis of a national dataset found, perhaps unsurprisingly, that negative communications about a child's behavior or learning did nothing to promote either school- or home-based engagement, while informative communication was strongly associated with higher family engagement. In the words of the researcher,

> If schools want to engage families on goals like improving academic achievement and behavior, then schools must understand that simply telling families that their children are having challenges in the classroom is not associated with increased family engagement. (Hine, 2022, p. 177)

New teachers can begin to build family communication streams through several pathways. Some elementary teachers offer a weekly digital newsletter to update families on what their child is learning. Teachers across grade levels can systematically make contact with each family throughout the year through phone calls or short written messages telling them something positive about their child. Secondary teachers can provide information about why their course is essential for post-secondary success. And all teachers can regularly provide tips to families about how to support children as they do their homework. (Hint: Make sure families don't think they need to do it for them!)

In Their Shoes

Teacher Credibility Leader Reflection

Directions: Instructional leaders, coaches, and mentors are not only effective because they bring a wealth of knowledge and experience to their role but also because they connect with their coachees' reality and recall how they felt when they were in the same position.

Since it may have been a few years since you were a first-year teacher, let's take a step back to remember and put ourselves in their shoes.

1. As a new teacher, which element of teacher credibility (trust, competence, dynamism, and immediacy) was your area of strength?

_____

_____

_____

_____

2. Which one of the four elements did you find most challenging? Why?

_____

_____

_____

_____

3. What do you understand about teacher credibility now, as an experienced educator, that you wish you knew back then?

_____

_____

_____

_____

(Continued)

(Continued)

4. Looking back, what coaching support did you receive? What do you wish you would have received?

_____

_____

_____

_____

_____

5. How will you incorporate your experience when onboarding your new teachers? How will you meet their needs?

_____

_____

_____

_____

_____

Coaching Scenario for Leaders

Ajay

Directions: Read the scenario below and consider what you would do as Ajay's instructional coach. Then answer the follow-up questions below.

You meet with Ajay in his classroom for the pre-observation meeting. You review the lesson plan together and hear him use the phrase "those kids." You notice that he continues to use that same terminology to describe students who "don't have the prerequisite skills," "don't care," or "don't have parents who care about their education." He expresses frustration with them and is not confident in being able to help them unless they switch to his remedial class.

Follow-Up Questions

1. What are your initial takeaways from listening to Ajay?

_____

_____

_____

_____

_____

2. What do his words reveal about the expectations that he has for students?

_____

_____

_____

_____

_____

3. What would your next steps be in coaching Ajay? What resources and ongoing support would you provide?

_____

_____

_____

_____

_____

Leaders Get Clear and Anticipate

With a strong onboarding process, instructional leaders and coaches send a clear message to new teachers about "how we do things." They communicate and reiterate the site's expectations around teaching and learning. This minimizes ambiguity so new teachers adapt and adopt best practices more quickly than if they were to navigate this theme on their own.

In Our Shoes

Teacher Credibility and High-Expectations
Teaching Leader Reflection

Directions: Instructional leaders, coaches, and mentors should pause first to get clear about their expectations. Then they can craft their message and provide onboarded teachers with appropriate feedback to elevate their practice.

1. What does teacher credibility look like at your school? How do you know if a teacher has high expectations for their students?

_____

_____

_____

_____

_____

2. What are three things that you want new teachers to know about teacher credibility and high-expectations teaching?

_____

_____

_____

_____

_____

3. What unique challenges do you anticipate new teachers will encounter?

_____

_____

_____

_____

_____

4. How will you customize your supports for each of your new teachers?

_____

_____

_____

_____

_____

In Our Shoes

Family Communications Leader Reflection

Directions: Instructional leaders, coaches, and mentors should pause first to get clear about their expectations. Then they can craft their message and provide onboarded teachers with appropriate feedback to elevate their practice.

1. What district or school procedures and guidelines exist for teacher communications with families? How will you ensure that new teachers are aware of them?

_____

_____

_____

_____

2. What are three things that you want new teachers to know about informative communication with families?

_____

_____

_____

_____

(Continued)

(Continued)

3. What unique challenges do you anticipate new teachers will encounter?

_____

_____

_____

_____

_____

4. What procedural guidelines exist as it applies to communication with families? Are there requirements about logging contact or receiving prior approval for written communications?

_____

_____

_____

_____

_____

5. What existing resources and expertise can new teachers draw from in proactive and positive family communications?

_____

_____

_____

_____

_____

Leaders Get Clear and Communicate

Now that you have a clear vision of this cycle's focus and what that looks like at your site, it is important to communicate this message along with your expectations. On the next page you will find a sample of an onboarding checklist with a suggested timeline for three groups of deliverables: Leader/Coach, New Teacher, and Together.

Onboarding Checklist

	LEADER/COACH	NEW TEACHER	TOGETHER
Week 1	Send a reminder email to new teachers about the upcoming monthly onboarding check-in meeting.	Complete the New Teachers Get Familiar and Implement interactions.	
	Put a note of appreciation in new teachers' office mailboxes. A handwritten note addressed to the new teacher will light up their day!		
	Complete the Context About the Theme section, including the interactions.		
	Complete the Leaders Get Clear and Anticipate section, including the interactions.		
	Review the Cycle 3 learning guide and slide deck at the companion website and make modifications as needed.		
	Invite expert teachers to join the onboarding meeting and share their best practices with new teachers. Ask them if they would welcome new teachers to visit their classrooms and ask for their availability.		
	Facilitate the monthly onboarding check-in meeting. This meeting is short (up to 30 minutes), and might occur before school, at lunch, or after school. We have provided a slide presentation for you to use and customize. Bring water and healthy snacks as tokens of appreciation.	Schedule time to visit an expert teacher's room. Complete the pre-work on the New Teachers Learn From Expert Teachers interactive feature.	Attend the monthly onboarding check-in meeting.
Week 2	Send a thank-you email to new teachers for attending the onboarding meeting. Confirm the dates for observation and post-observation meetings via calendar invites. Send a thank-you email to the expert teachers who attended the onboarding meeting and invite new teachers to visit their classrooms.	Visit the expert teacher's classroom. Use the New Teachers Learn From Expert Teachers interactive feature to document your learning. Thank the expert teacher in person or by email for inviting you into their classroom.	Schedule classroom observation focused on the theme. Agree on a data collection tool. Schedule post-observation meeting.

(Continued)

(Continued)

	LEADER/COACH	NEW TEACHER	TOGETHER
Week 3	Review the New Teachers Get Familiar and Implement section, including interactions.		Conduct classroom observation. Hold the post-observation meeting with a debrief tool.
Week 4	Give them an end-of-the-month token of appreciation to congratulate them on successfully completing another month.	Complete the Check-In and Follow-Up tools for interactions.	
	Review and reflect on responses from submitted Leaders Ask "How Did We Do?" surveys.		
	Complete the Trust Recalibration interaction. Send a reminder email about next month's onboarding meeting (date, time, location). Include calendar invites.		

Email to New Teachers on the First Day of Cycle

(Example)

Hello _____,

I hope you are feeling proud of your accomplishments during this first quarter of the school year. Please know that our continued support of your professional development is important to all of us at school.

As we begin the next chapter of our learning, I want to invite you again to our next onboarding meeting on _____ on teacher credibility, high expectations, and family communications. We have so many expert teachers on our staff, and I know you will learn after they share their best practices around our focus area. I encourage you to prepare thoughts and wonderings beforehand so we can have dialogue around our practice.

I look forward to working with you as the year continues. We are so lucky to have you on our team!

Sincerely,

_____

(Other Conversations to Consider)

- District and schoolwide committee meetings
- District and schoolwide professional development opportunities
- Local and community events
- Staff socials and events
- Student events:
  - Theater performances
  - Chorus concerts
  - Band and orchestra concerts
  - Dance competitions
  - Athletic events, games, tournaments
  - School fundraisers
  - School dances

Invitational Email to Expert Teachers

(Example)

Hello _____,

As you know, we have _____ new teachers who joined our team. My goal is to work closely with them throughout the year and to support their transition through an onboarding process. For the next several weeks, we will be focused on teacher credibility, high-expectations teaching, and family communications. I will offer resources and ongoing support, but they also asked for my help in identifying expert teachers in these areas, so naturally I thought of you.

Our next onboarding meeting is on _____. Our new teachers want and need to see best practices in action to grow professionally. I have no doubt that they would benefit so much from hearing about what you do, how you do it, lessons learned, and any other words of wisdom you are willing to share. I've attached a brief summary of the topics we are spotlighting this month [attach the Context About the Theme found at the beginning of this cycle]. Would you be willing to join us at our onboarding meeting and open your classroom doors so new teachers can learn from you?

Thank you for mentoring the next generation of educators!

Sincerely,

_____

Leaders Express Appreciation

Here is a checklist of ways that leaders/coaches can show a token of their appreciation to new teachers for all of their hard work. This could also show your teachers how to pay it forward. Showing them graciousness will move them to show and connect with their students. We recommend that you do one item from this checklist this month to make them feel welcome and a part of the school.

(Examples)

Write a one- or two-sentence message on a thank-you card. Put it in their office mailbox with a special treat:

[School or district swag]

- Lanyards
- T-shirts or sweaters from student council or ASB
- Accessories like scarves, hats, socks, etc.
- Pencils, mugs, tumblers, etc. with the school or district logo

Expert Tip: Check if there are forgotten items from previous years in the site or district supply rooms.

[Items they may need in their classrooms]

- Tissue
- Pencils or pens
- Paper
- Wipes
- Whiteboard markers
- Smelly markers
- Composition notebooks
- Gift baskets of supplies

Expert Tip: Ask parent/family groups, community members, or local businesses for donations.

[Other gift ideas]

- Gently used novels
- Reusable shopping bags or canvas tote bags
- Boxed thank-you cards

New Teachers Get Familiar and Implement

Video Reflection
Invest in Your Credibility

Directions: Let's look at an eleventh-grade teacher and analyze how she invests in her credibility. Do not be distracted by her content or grade level. Focus on how she fosters her credibility (trustworthiness, competence, dynamism, immediacy). After watching Video 3.1 (available at the companion website), answer each question below.

1. In what ways does the teacher show herself to be trustworthy (benevolent and reliable)?

_____

_____

_____

_____

2. In what ways does the teacher show herself to be competent (knows her content)?

_____

_____

_____

_____

3. In what ways does the teacher show herself to be dynamic (enthusiastic about her content and her students)?

_____

_____

_____

_____

4. In what ways does the teacher show herself to be responsive and immediate?

_____

_____

_____

_____

Video Reflection

Investing in One's Credibility

Directions: Now watch the same video (available at the companion website) a second time, this time through the lens of high-expectations teaching. Again, do not be distracted by whether her content or grade level is different from your own. You are developing your expert noticing skills. Use the checklist to note how many of these high-expectations teaching moves you have seen (you will not see them all in a single video).

After re-watching Video 3.1, answer each question below.

1. List the high-expectations teaching moves you saw in this video.

_____

_____

_____

_____

_____

2. What were the actions and reactions of her students?

_____

_____

_____

_____

3. What were your observations about the level of cognitive engagement among students?

_____

_____

_____

_____

New Teachers Self-Assess

Teacher Credibility

Directions: Take a moment to assess yourself in the area of teacher credibility.

1. What do you specifically do or say to show students that you are trustworthy and reliable?

   _____

   _____

   _____

   _____

   _____

2. Do you demonstrate competency? Why or why not?

   _____

   _____

   _____

   _____

   _____

3. Are you a dynamic teacher? Provide examples.

   _____

   _____

   _____

   _____

4. How do you demonstrate immediacy with students?

   _____

   _____

   _____

   _____

   _____

New Teachers Self-Assess

High-Expectations Teaching

Directions: Use Figure 3.2 to assess yourself in the area of high-expectations teaching. Some of these are not manifested within a single lesson but are utilized weekly. Where do you need to increase the frequency and quality of your interactions? What are you doing well?

Figure 3.2 Self-Assessment: Are You a High-Expectations Teacher?

Directions: Use the following self-assessment checklist to identify the frequency of the high-expectation practices that you use.

HOW OFTEN DO YOU USE THE FOLLOWING HIGH-EXPECTATION PRACTICES IN YOUR TEACHING?	RARELY	SOMETIMES	OFTEN
Ask open questions.			
Praise effort rather than correct answers.			
Use regular formative assessment.			
Rephrase questions when answers are incorrect.			
Use mixed-ability groupings.			
Change groupings regularly.			
Encourage students to work with a range of their peers.			
Provide a range of activities.			
Allow students to choose their own activities from a range of options.			
Make explicit learning intentions and success criteria.			

HOW OFTEN DO YOU USE THE FOLLOWING HIGH-EXPECTATION PRACTICES IN YOUR TEACHING?	RARELY	SOMETIMES	OFTEN
Allow students to contribute to success criteria.			
Give students responsibility for their learning.			
Get to know each student personally.			
Incorporate students' interests into activities.			
Establish routines and procedures at the beginning of the school year.			
Work with students to set individual goals.			
Teach students about SMART (specific, measurable, achievable, relevant, and time-bound) goals.			
Regularly review goals with students.			
Link achievement to motivation, effort, and goal setting.			
Minimize differentiation in activities between high and low achievers.			
Allow all learners to engage in advanced activities.			

(Continued)

(Continued)

HOW OFTEN DO YOU USE THE FOLLOWING HIGH-EXPECTATION PRACTICES IN YOUR TEACHING?	RARELY	SOMETIMES	OFTEN
Give specific instructional feedback about students' achievement in relation to learning goals.			
Take a facilitative role and support students to make choices about their learning.			
Manage behavior positively and proactively.			
Work with all students equally.			

Source: Hargraves (2018, https://theeducationhub.org.nz/high-expectations-self-assessment-check list). Developed from Rubie-Davies (2014).

Your Turn

Practice Planning for High-Expectations Teaching

Directions: Find a lesson plan that you will implement with your students. Use the prompts to analyze how you communicate a high level of expectations and make adjustments as needed.

	YES	NO	REFLECTION
1. Is there a time when you explicitly teach the learning intentions and success criteria?			
2. Have you planned open questions?			

	YES	NO	REFLECTION
3. Will students work in mixed-ability groups?			
4. Are you minimizing differentiation in activities between high- and low-achieving students?			
5. Are students able to exercise choice and decision making to promote ownership of learning?			
6. Have you planned opportunities to give and receive feedback?			
7. Have you incorporated student interests into the lesson?			
8. Have you planned for ways to check for understanding?			

Your Turn

Practice Family Communications With a Student Praise Report

What better way is there to show that we care about our students than to brag about how wonderful they are to their families? Parents and caregivers believe teachers are credible when they know that the adults at school see their whole child. This establishes a trusting relationship with families, who are more willing and able to become partners with you.

Directions: Think of ten students who you know would appreciate getting a positive call home. Don't limit these contacts to those who historically do well in school. Consider individuals who might be in need of a little extra care and positivity. Continue this practice by making at least five student praise reports per week. Keep track of your contacts to ensure you aren't overlooking anyone.

(Continued)

(Continued)

Note: It is more convenient to send an email than to make a phone call, but which one would make a stronger impact? If you were on the receiving end, which one would you prefer?

STUDENT NAME	REASON(S) FOR PRAISE REPORT	DATE/TIME
1.		
2.		
3.		
4.		
5.		
6.		
7.		
8.		
9.		
10.		

Reflection

After you made contact with families, did you notice anything different with the student? If so, what changes did you notice?

_____

_____

_____

_____

_____

Check-In and Follow-Up Tools for Leaders

New teachers need and appreciate low-stakes timely feedback. Arrange a short visit with the new teacher (10 to 15 minutes) and provide information about what you saw and heard and what questions you have to continue the conversation. This check-in tool is not a formal observation. Rather, it is a means to monitor learning and development related to high-expectations teaching.

Classroom Observation Tool

High-Expectations Teaching

Learning Intention			
Success Criteria			
	YES	**NOT OBSERVED**	**EVIDENCE**
1. Learning intentions and success criteria explicitly taught?			

(Continued)

(Continued)

	YES	NOT OBSERVED	EVIDENCE
2. Open questions posed?			
3. Students working in mixed-ability groups?			
4. Activities minimizing differentiation between high- and low-achieving students?			
5. Students exercise choice and decision making to promote ownership of learning?			
6. Opportunities to give and receive feedback?			
7. Student interests incorporated?			
8. Ways to check for understanding?			

Post-Observation Debrief

High-Expectations Teaching

Learning Intention	
Success Criteria	
	EVIDENCE
Emerging Patterns and Trends	
What do you feel worked well? Why?	
What does a successful lesson look like and sound like to you?	

(Continued)

(Continued)

	EVIDENCE
What are you most afraid of? Why?	
What is a near-term goal you have for yourself?	
What is a near-term goal you have with your students?	
What might help you reach your near-term goals for yourself and your students?	

New teachers are eager to collaborate with colleagues, so the onboarding process offers them opportunities to do this. One of the ways that they can develop professionally is by working with expert teachers and visiting their classrooms. Instructional leaders, coaches, and mentors play a pivotal role in connecting them to mentor teachers who add to their collegial network.

New Teachers Learn From Expert Teachers

Teacher Credibility and High-Expectations Teaching

Directions: You have an amazing opportunity to collaborate with and visit an expert teacher on your site. This tool is designed to ensure that you have a learning experience that will directly impact your practice with your students.

Pre-Visit Preparation

Before visiting the classroom, what are three questions that you want to ask the expert teacher related to teacher credibility or high-expectations teaching? Capture their responses below.

QUESTIONS	ANSWERS

Look-Fors During the Visit

What three elements are you looking for or hoping to see? Document evidence of those look-fors below.

LOOK-FORS (TEACHER CREDIBILITY AND HIGH-EXPECTATIONS TEACHING)	EVIDENCE

(Continued)

(Continued)

Post-Visit Reflection
Reflect on the visit to the expert teacher's classroom. Answer each question below.
1. How will this visit support your growth as a new and effective teacher?
2. What specific strategies or tools will you take back to your classroom?
3. Do you have any follow-up questions that you would like to ask the expert teacher?
Expert Tip: Send the expert teacher a thank-you email and include what you enjoyed about their classroom and how visiting them made you a better teacher!

Leaders Cycle Back With New Teachers

Thank you for your tireless commitment to our students! As we move forward through our progressions, it is important to revisit what we learned previously so we don't forget and continue to grow in those areas.
Directions: Read the list of previous themes. Select one and answer the questions below.
Previous Theme(s) • Setting up the physical classroom, routines, and procedures • Invitational teaching, student engagement, universal classroom management
1. What new takeaways or aha moments have you encountered since we last reviewed this topic?
2. In what ways have you continued to develop professionally in this area?

3. What lingering questions or wonderings do you have for a leader, coach, or expert teacher?

Leaders Ask "How Did We Do?"

Teacher Credibility and High-Expectations Teaching

It is very important for me to gauge my effectiveness as a coach because I want to provide a productive work environment. Please help me in meeting this goal.

Using the following scale, with 1 being not confident, 3 being somewhat confident, and 5 indicating very confident, how confident are you in your ability to do the following as it relates to teacher credibility, high-expectations teaching, and family communication?

Thank you for all that you do!

"I know where I'm going." I understand my current performance and how it relates to my professional growth.	 Please elaborate:
"I have the tools for the journey." I understand that I can select from a range of strategies to move my learning forward, especially when progress is interrupted.	 Please elaborate:
"I monitor my progress." I seek and respond to feedback from others to assess my own performance. I know that making mistakes is expected and indicates an opportunity for further learning.	 Please elaborate:
"I recognize when I'm ready for what's next." I make my own observations to identify when I'm ready to move on.	 Please elaborate:

(Continued)

(Continued)

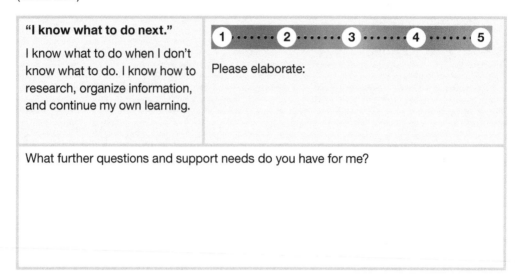

| "I know what to do next."

I know what to do when I don't know what to do. I know how to research, organize information, and continue my own learning. | 1 · · · · · 2 · · · · · 3 · · · · · 4 · · · · · 5

Please elaborate: |

What further questions and support needs do you have for me?

Tying It Together With Trust

Recall the five facets of trustworthiness in leaders (benevolence, reliability, competence, honesty, and openness) from page 34. Consider taking a moment to pause and reflect on your behaviors and interactions with your staff during the last few weeks:

> In what ways did you develop trust specifically with new teachers?

> Were there any instances in which you unintentionally acted in a way that might have resulted in lowering their trust?

> As we move into the next month, what will you continue doing? What will you start doing? What will you stop doing?

Trust Recalibration

Looking Back to Move Forward

	EVIDENCE OF TRUSTING BEHAVIORS	EVIDENCE OF DISTRUSTING BEHAVIORS	HOW WILL I MAINTAIN OR DEVELOP TRUST NEXT MONTH?
(1) Benevolence			
(2) Reliability			
(3) Competence			
(4) Honesty			
(5) Openness			

Conclusion

In this cycle, we introduced teacher credibility, teacher expectations teaching, and family communication. These concepts are important to address in the onboarding process because they highlight student–teacher relationships. Beliefs and perceptions about the teacher directly impact student learning and well-being. Families also benefit from teacher credibility and high-expectations teaching. They advocate for their children and want them to experience the best education. Families deserve to have it delivered by educators they trust.

Additional Resources

For Leaders and Coaches

Fisher, D., Frey, N., Lassiter, C., & Smith, D. (2022). *Leader credibility: The essential traits of those who engage, inspire, and transform.* Corwin.

A 4-Minute Read for New Teachers

Kreisberg, H. (2022, January 11). 3 tips to enhance communication with families. *Corwin Connect.* https://corwin-connect.com/2022/01/3-tips-to-enhance-communication-with-families-about-their-childs-math-before-years-end/

A 5-Minute Read for Expert Teachers

Napper, K. (2019, June 26). The necessity of having high expectations. *Edutopia.* https://www.edutopia.org/article/necessity-having-high-expectations/

Visit the companion website at
https://qrs.ly/9mesfwe
for additional resources.

CYCLE 4
ARE WE TEACHING WITH CLARITY?
(4 WEEKS)

In This Section

- Teacher Clarity

- Learning Intentions

- Relevance

- Success Criteria

Context About the Theme of Teaching With Clarity

This cycle's theme is about teaching with clarity. As with previous themes, we acknowledge that this topic cannot be fully "taught" for four weeks. Having said that, we invite you to link this to existing initiatives regarding teacher clarity. Your district may use slightly different terminology—learning targets, learning objectives, and such. We encourage you to use the prevailing language of your educational community so as not to unnecessarily confuse new teachers.

Students succeed when they have a clear understanding of what they are expected to learn, why they are learning it, and how they will know that they have learned it. In other words, an effective teacher is one who demystifies the learning process and exemplifies teacher clarity. Teacher clarity is "a measure of the clarity of communication between teachers and students in both directions" (Fendick, 1990) and it has four dimensions (see Figure 4.1). It has an overall effect size of 0.85, so it makes sense that instructional leaders and coaches select this as a top focus for schoolwide instructional improvement by way of learning intentions (Visible Learning Meta[X], 2021).

Figure 4.1   Four Dimensions of Teacher Clarity

1. **Clarity of organization,** such that lesson tasks, assignments, and activities include links to the objectives and outcomes of learning.

2. **Clarity of explanation,** such that information is relevant, accurate, and comprehensible to students.

3. **Clarity of examples and guided practice,** such that the lesson includes information that is illustrative and illuminating as students gradually move to independence, making progress with less support from the teacher.

4. **Clarity of assessment of student learning,** such that the teacher is regularly seeking out and acting upon the feedback he or she receives from students, especially through their verbal and written responses.

Source: Fisher, Frey, Amador, and Assof (2018, p. xiv).

Student Ownership of Learning

We all want students to take ownership of their learning. But this is made much more difficult if we keep them in the dark about what they are learning, why they are learning it, and how they will know they have learned it. In fact, these are the three driving questions that, if addressed, can elevate students from low-level compliance to owning their learning (see Figure 4.2).

Figure 4.2   Questions and Answers for Students and Teachers

QUESTIONS LEARNERS HAVE	ANSWERS TEACHERS CAN PROVIDE
What am I learning?	Learning Intentions
Why am I learning it?	Relevance
How will I know I have learned it?	Success Criteria

Teachers invite students to take ownership of their learning experience by making it visible through learning intentions, statements of relevance, and success criteria. Learning intentions have an effect size of 0.54 and help them address the "what are we expected to learn" question (Visible Learning Meta[X], 2021):

▸ We're learning about energy in different phases of matter.

▸ We're learning about how to write an opinion paragraph.

Addressing relevance situates their learning in the context of usefulness and, in some cases, contributes to the building of one's identities. For instance, the learning on a particular day may be about personal usefulness:

▸ We're learning about energy in different phases of matter so that you can understand how the movement of molecules changes.

In a different lesson, it may be about one's identities:

▸ We are learning about how to write an opinion paragraph so that you can explain your opinion and convince others.

Success criteria round out these three questions and seek to address the question, "How will I know I have learned it?" Success criteria have an effect size of 0.88 (Visible Learning Meta[X], 2021) and are widely used in business, construction, and project management precisely because they accelerate productivity and increase the likelihood of successful outcomes. There are a number of different ways to establish criteria for success, including rubrics and scaled student exemplars. One popular method is to use I-can statements:

▸ I can explain the relationship between pressure, temperature, and states of matter.

Another way is to equip the student with a way to utilize feedback to gauge their success:

▸ I'll know that I have learned it when my reader can explain my opinion after reading my paragraph.

It is not enough for students to base their learning on whether or not they completed a task, such as an essay, presentation, or worksheet, which reinforces compliance rather than learning. Sharing success criteria means students have ways to check their progress based on their understanding of the knowledge, skills, and concepts articulated in the learning intentions. Other examples of success criteria in the form of I-can statements can be found in Figure 4.3.

Figure 4.3   Success Criteria: I-Can Examples

English Language Arts	• I will be able to clearly support my opinion using evidence from the text. • I can use correct spelling and punctuation so my reader can understand my writing. • I am able to explain Poe's use of the unreliable narrator in short stories. • My story has an opening that grabs the reader's attention and an ending with a cliffhanger.
Mathematics	• I can put numbers with decimals in order from smallest to largest. • I can identify all prime numbers between 1 and 100. • I can make a table of equivalent ratios. • I can explain why two fractions are equivalent. • I can explain how to locate the solution to a system of equations by examining a graph.
Science	• I can show how buoyancy and density affect an object suspended in a liquid. • I can name the planets of the solar system in order of their distance from the sun. • I can explain how changes in velocity affect the movement of an object.
Social Studies	• I can compare and contrast how people traveled long ago and today. • I can identify when, how, and why this country was established. • I can define the necessary conditions for an economy to grow.

Source: Fisher, Frey, Amador, and Assof (2018, p. 31).

In Their Shoes

Teacher Clarity Leader Reflection

Directions: Instructional leaders, coaches, and mentors are not only effective because they bring a wealth of knowledge and experience to their role, but also because they connect with their coachees' reality and recall how they felt when they were in the same position.

If you have been in education for a while, chances are good that teacher clarity was not commonly taught in your preparation program, although the research on it dates back more than half a century. Let's take a step back to remember and put ourselves in their shoes.

1. Which of the four dimensions of teacher clarity (organization, explanation, examples and guided practice, and assessment of student learning), did you do well? Explain.

_____

_____

_____

_____

_____

2. Which dimension(s) were more challenging in your first year? Why?

_____

_____

_____

_____

_____

3. What do you know now, as an experienced educator, that you wish you knew back then, as a new teacher?

_____

_____

_____

_____

_____

4. Looking back, what coaching support did you receive? What do you wish you would have received?

_____

_____

_____

_____

_____

5. How will you incorporate your experience when developing your instructional coaching plan? How will you meet the needs of new teachers?

_____

_____

_____

_____

_____

Coaching Scenario for Leaders

Sonia

Directions: Read the scenario below and consider what you would do as Sonia's instructional coach. Then answer the follow-up questions below.

Sonia asked you to visit her class because she is excited to introduce a hands-on project with students this week. As promised, you enter the classroom the next day and observe students huddled in groups. Students are excited and engaged, and then you recall having seen this activity before. You observed it earlier in the year in another teacher's class, with students two grade levels below.

You visit with each group to probe their thinking. You ask them three questions ("What are you learning?," "Why are you learning it?," and "How will you know when you have learned it?") and discover that two out of five groups answered all three questions but only one answered them correctly. The remaining three groups provided responses related to the project, but not the learning intention or success criteria written on the board. Students are excited and engaged, but you start to wonder if the activity is aligned to the grade-level standards.

Follow-Up Questions

1. What does the data reveal about the alignment between teacher clarity, student engagement, and standards-based instruction?

_____

_____

_____

_____

_____

2. What questions might you ask Sonia about teacher clarity in the post-observation debrief?

_____

_____

_____

_____

_____

3. What would your next steps be in coaching Sonia? What resources and ongoing support would you provide?

_____

_____

_____

_____

_____

Leaders Get Clear and Anticipate

With a strong onboarding process, instructional leaders and coaches send a clear message to new teachers about "how we do things." They communicate and reiterate the site's expectations around how student ownership is fostered. This minimizes ambiguity so new teachers adapt and adopt best practices more quickly than if they were to navigate this theme on their own.

In Our Shoes

Teacher Clarity Leader Reflection

Directions: Instructional leaders, coaches, and mentors should pause first to get clear about their expectations. Then they can craft their message and provide onboarded teachers with appropriate feedback to elevate their practice.

1. What professional learning opportunities has the site had about teaching with clarity?

_____

_____

_____

_____

_____

(Continued)

(Continued)

2. Are there schoolwide expectations related to the use of learning intentions and success criteria? What are they?

_____

_____

_____

_____

_____

3. Think about the last time you visited classrooms. What percent of the current staff utilized learning intentions and success criteria with students?

_____

_____

_____

_____

_____

4. What unique challenges do you anticipate new teachers will encounter?

_____

_____

_____

_____

_____

5. How will you customize your supports for each of your new teachers?

_____

_____

_____

_____

_____

Leaders Get Clear and Communicate

Now that you have a clear vision of this cycle's focus and what that looks like at your site, it is important to communicate this message along with your expectations. Below you will find a sample of an onboarding checklist with a suggested timeline for three groups of deliverables Leader/Coach, New Teacher, and Together.

Onboarding Checklist

	LEADER/COACH	NEW TEACHER	TOGETHER
Week 1	Send a reminder email to new teachers about the upcoming monthly onboarding check-in meeting.	Complete the New Teachers Get Familiar and Implement interactions.	
	Put a note of appreciation in new teachers' office mailboxes. A handwritten note addressed to the new teacher will light up their day!		
	Complete the Context About the Theme section, including the interactions.		
	Complete the Leaders Get Clear and Anticipate section, including the interactions.		
	Review the Cycle 4 learning guide and slide deck at the companion website and make modifications as needed.		
	Invite expert teachers to join the onboarding meeting and share their best practices with new teachers. Ask them if they would welcome new teachers to visit their classrooms and ask for their availability.		
	Facilitate the monthly onboarding check-in meeting. This meeting is short (up to 30 minutes), and might occur before school, at lunch, or after school. We have provided a slide presentation for you to use and customize. Bring water and healthy snacks as tokens of appreciation.	Schedule time to visit an expert teacher's room. Complete the pre-work on the New Teachers Learn From Expert Teachers interactive feature.	Attend the monthly onboarding check-in meeting.

(Continued)

(Continued)

	LEADER/COACH	NEW TEACHER	TOGETHER
		Visit the expert teacher's classroom. Use the New Teachers Learn From Expert Teachers interactive feature to document your learning. Thank the expert teacher in person or by email for inviting you into their classroom.	Schedule classroom observation focused on the theme. Agree on a data collection tool. Schedule post-observation meeting.
Week 2	Send a thank-you email to new teachers for attending the onboarding meeting. Confirm the dates for observation and post-observation meetings via calendar invites. Send a thank-you email to the expert teachers who attended the onboarding meeting and invite new teachers to visit their classrooms.		
Week 3	Review the New Teachers Get Familiar and Implement section, including interactions.		Conduct classroom observation. Hold the post-observation meeting with a debrief tool.
Week 4	Give them an end-of-the-month token of appreciation to congratulate them on successfully completing another month.	Complete the Check-In and Follow-Up tools for interactions.	
	Review and reflect on responses from submitted Leaders Ask "How Did We Do?" surveys.		
	Complete the Trust Recalibration interaction.		
	Send a reminder email about next month's onboarding meeting (date, time, location). Include calendar invites.		

Email to New Teachers on the First Day of Cycle

(Example)

Hello _____,

Can you believe we're already in the month of _____? Time flies by so fast!

As we begin the next chapter of our learning, I want to invite you again to our next onboarding meeting on _____ on teacher clarity. I invited more expert teachers to share their best practices around developing effective learning intentions and success criteria, so this is our chance to pick their brains and visit their classrooms. Feel free to come with questions and be ready to share.

I have enjoyed getting to know you and I appreciate everything that you do to support our students and their families.

Sincerely,

_____

(Other Conversations to Consider)

- District and schoolwide committee meetings
- District and schoolwide professional development opportunities
- Local and community events
- Staff socials and events
- Student events:
  - Theater performances
  - Chorus concerts
  - Band and orchestra concerts
  - Dance competitions
  - Athletic events, games, tournaments
  - School fundraisers
  - School dances

Invitational Email to Expert Teachers

(Example)

Hello _____,

I hope you had a great weekend and got a chance to disconnect and do something fun!

As you know, we have _____ new teachers who joined our team. My goal is to work closely with them throughout the year and to support their transition through an onboarding process. For the next several weeks, we will be focused on aspects of teacher clarity, specifically learning intentions, relevance, and success criteria. I have attached a summary of this cycle's theme [attach the Context About the Theme found at the beginning of this cycle]. I will offer resources and ongoing support, but they also asked for my help in identifying expert teachers in these areas, so naturally I thought of you.

Our next onboarding meeting is on _____. Our new teachers want to see best practices in action and would benefit so much from hearing about what you do, how you do it, lessons learned, and any other words of wisdom you are willing to share. Would you be willing to open your classroom doors so new teachers can learn from you?

I hope you will come join us so we can build community and share experiences and best practices.

Thank you for shaping the next generation of educators!

Sincerely,

_____

Leaders Express Appreciation

Here is a checklist of ways that leaders/coaches can show a token of their appreciation to new teachers for all of their hard work. This could also show your teachers how to pay it forward. Showing them graciousness will move them to show and connect with their students. We recommend that you do one item from this checklist this month to make them feel welcome and a part of the school.

(Examples)

Write a one- or two-sentence message on a thank-you card. Put it in their office mailbox with a special treat:

[School or district swag]

- Lanyards

- T-shirts or sweaters from student council or ASB

- Accessories like scarves, hats, socks, etc.

- Pencils, mugs, tumblers, etc. with the school or district logo

Expert Tip: Check if there are forgotten items from previous years in the site or district supply rooms.

[Items they may need in their classrooms]

- Tissue
- Pencils or pens
- Paper
- Wipes
- Whiteboard markers
- Smelly markers
- Composition notebooks
- Gift baskets of supplies

Expert Tip: Ask parent/family groups, community members, or local businesses for donations.

[Other gift ideas]

- Gently used novels
- Reusable shopping bags or canvas tote bags
- Boxed thank-you cards

New Teachers Get Familiar and Implement

Video Reflection

Teach With Clarity

Directions: Let's look at a fourth-grade teacher and analyze how she uses learning intentions and success criteria to set the stage for learning. Do not be distracted by her content or grade level. You are developing your expert noticing. After watching Video 4.1 (available at the companion website), answer each question below.

1. In what ways does the teacher teach and use (not just post) her learning goals and success criteria?

_____

_____

_____

_____

_____

(Continued)

(Continued)

2. In what ways does the teacher utilize the goals throughout the lesson?

_____

_____

_____

_____

_____

3. In what ways do students appear to use the learning goals and success criteria?

_____

_____

_____

_____

_____

4. How do self-assessment opportunities increase student ownership of learning?

_____

_____

_____

_____

5. How does the teacher gauge her students' progress to determine learning?

_____

_____

_____

_____

_____

6. Use what you know: What is the effect of well-established routines and procedures on her lesson?

_____

_____

_____

_____

_____

7. Use what you know: What high-expectations teaching practices did you see?

_____

_____

_____

_____

_____

Video Reflection

A Teacher Thinks Aloud About Learning Intentions and Success Criteria

Directions: Let's look at a sixth-grade English teacher as she explains her team's process for developing learning intentions and success criteria. Do not be distracted by her content or grade level. You are developing your expert noticing. She begins by deconstructing a standard to highlight concepts and skills. Next, she discusses the learning progressions needed. She ends by thinking aloud about her learning intentions and success criteria and the meaningful learning experiences she will design for her students. After watching Video 4.2 (available at the companion website), answer each question below.

1. What are the advantages of using nouns and verbs to deconstruct a standard?

_____

_____

_____

_____

_____

(Continued)

2. According to the teacher, what is the range of how long can a learning progression take?

_____

_____

_____

_____

_____

3. What learning intention does she discuss? Write it below.

_____

_____

_____

_____

_____

4. The teacher develops four success criteria, which will be introduced over several lessons. List them below.

- _____

- _____

- _____

- _____

- _____

5. What meaningful learning experiences does she explain?

_____

_____

_____

_____

_____

6. Use what you know: How does this process support efforts to teach with high expectations?

_____

_____

_____

_____

_____

New Teachers Self-Assess

Teaching With Clarity

Directions: Take a moment to assess yourself about the development and use of learning intentions and success criteria. This will help me in designing supports for you.

1. On a scale of 1 to 5 (with 1 being least and 5 being most), how confident are you in the development of learning intentions?

_____

_____

_____

_____

_____

2. On a scale of 1 to 5 (with 1 being least and 5 being most), how confident are you in developing success criteria for your lessons?

_____

_____

_____

_____

_____

(Continued)

(Continued)

3. On a scale of 1 to 5 (with 1 being least and 5 being most), how confident are you in locating and utilizing district/site resources to assist you in developing these?

_____

_____

_____

_____

_____

4. On a scale of 1 to 5 (with 1 being least and 5 being most), how confident are you in using these in your own lessons?

_____

_____

_____

_____

_____

5. What support and coaching do you need to continue your growth?

_____

_____

_____

_____

_____

Your Turn

Practice Teaching With Clarity

Look at a lesson you are currently developing for use in the near future. As you examine your developing lesson, use these questions to guide your planning. Once you have taught this lesson, debrief the experience with your coach or mentor.

Lesson Planning Tool

Teacher Clarity

What do you want students to learn in this lesson? (*Learning Intention:* These are skills and concepts, not tasks)	
What does success look like or sound like? (*Success Criteria:* These are measures of success, not completion of a task)	
	MY EVIDENCE
Clarity of Organization What experiences and tasks will students engage in to achieve the lesson's learning intention?	
Clarity of Explanation Are the explanations accurate? Are they developmentally appropriate? Do they foster relevancy? Are they anchored to prior knowledge?	

(Continued)

(Continued)

	MY EVIDENCE
Clarity of Examples and Guided Practice What examples and non-examples will you use to illuminate the skills or concepts you are teaching toward? How will students have opportunities to apply these skills and concepts in the company of peers?	
Clarity of Assessment of Student Learning How will you check for understanding? How will the tasks help you to do so? What questions do you want to ask? How will you assess whether they have learned it?	

Check-In and Follow-Up Tools for Leaders

Host capacity-building learning walks with new teachers during this cycle. Volunteer teachers open up their classrooms for short, pre-arranged observations (about 10 minutes) for a pre-determined area of focus, in this case, teaching with clarity. An administrator, coach, or mentor can host the learning walk. Observers are divided into three teams (A, B, and C), and have a specific task to conduct in each classroom. The observers debrief after three classroom visits, and the discussion is confined to patterns gleaned, not about individual classrooms. The composition of the team rotates so that observers have the experience of collecting data across all three sources (teacher, students, and environment). The team debrief of the experience is conducted at the end to draw conclusions.

New teachers may not fully understand the difference between observing for patterns and evaluation. Discourage them from using evaluative statements (e.g., "I liked the way . . ." or "The teacher should have . . ."). Instead, remind them to use objective statements (e.g., "Three students described . . ." or "Two of the three classrooms posted learning intentions and success criteria"). In addition, remind them of the focus: teaching with clarity. Don't get distracted by the other things that might be occurring!

Capacity-Building Learning Walk Tool

Focus on Teaching With Clarity

WHAT IS THE *TEACHER* DOING AS IT RELATES TO TEACHER CLARITY?	HOW DO *STUDENTS* DESCRIBE THEIR LEARNING? *"WHAT ARE YOU LEARNING TODAY?"* *"WHY ARE YOU LEARNING IT?"* *"HOW WILL YOU KNOW YOU HAVE LEARNED IT?"*	HOW DOES THE *ENVIRONMENT* SUPPORT THE LEARNING AS IT RELATES TO TEACHER CLARITY?
Classroom 1: Time:		
Classroom 2: Time:		
Classroom 3: Time:		

Debrief on Patterns After Three Classrooms

	TEAM A REPORTS ON WHAT THE *TEACHERS* WERE DOING, AS IT RELATES TO TEACHER CLARITY.	TEAM B REPORTS ON HOW *STUDENTS* DESCRIBED THEIR LEARNING.	TEAM C REPORTS ON THE WAYS IN WHICH THE *ENVIRONMENT* SUPPORTED THE LEARNING, AS IT RELATES TO TEACHER CLARITY.
Emerging Patterns and Trends			

(Continued)

(Continued)

	TEAM A REPORTS ON WHAT THE *TEACHERS* WERE DOING, AS IT RELATES TO TEACHER CLARITY.	TEAM B REPORTS ON HOW *STUDENTS* DESCRIBED THEIR LEARNING.	TEAM C REPORTS ON THE WAYS IN WHICH THE *ENVIRONMENT* SUPPORTED THE LEARNING, AS IT RELATES TO TEACHER CLARITY.
What conclusions can be drawn for use in our own classrooms?			
What growth opportunities can we identify for ourselves?			
In what ways was this process helpful or not helpful? **How can I better support you?**			

Source: Adapted from Fisher et al. (2019, pp. 90–92).

New teachers are eager to collaborate with colleagues, so the onboarding process offers them opportunities to do this. One of the ways that they can develop professionally is by working with expert teachers and visiting their classrooms. Instructional leaders and coaches play a pivotal role in connecting them to mentor teachers who add to their collegial network.

New Teachers Learn From Expert Teachers

Teacher Clarity

Directions: You have an amazing opportunity to collaborate with and visit an expert teacher on your site. This tool is designed to ensure that you have a learning experience that will directly impact your practice with your students.

Pre-Visit Preparation

Before visiting the classroom, what are three questions that you want to ask the expert teacher related to teaching with clarity? Capture their responses below.

QUESTIONS	ANSWERS

Look-Fors During the Visit

What three elements are you looking for or hoping to see? Document evidence of those look-fors below.

LOOK-FORS (TEACHER CLARITY)	EVIDENCE

(Continued)

(Continued)

Post-Visit Reflection

Reflect on the visit to the expert teacher's classroom. Answer each question below.

1. How will this visit support your growth as a new and effective teacher?

2. What specific strategies or tools will you take back to your classroom?

3. Do you have any follow-up questions that you would like to ask the expert teacher?

Expert Tip: Send the expert teacher a thank-you email and include what you enjoyed about their classroom and how visiting them made you a better teacher!

Leaders Cycle Back With New Teachers

Thank you for your commitment to our students! As we move forward through our progressions, it is important to revisit what we learned previously so we don't forget and continue to grow in those areas.

Directions: Read the list of previous themes. Select one and answer the questions below.

Previous Theme(s)

- Setting up the physical classroom, routines, and procedures
- Student engagement and classroom management
- Teacher credibility, teacher expectations, and family communication

1. What new takeaways or aha moments did you encounter?

2. In what ways did teaching with clarity intersect with your prior knowledge about the theme you selected?

3. What lingering questions or wonderings do you have for a leader, coach, or expert teacher?

Leaders Ask "How Did We Do?"

Teacher Clarity

It is very important for me to gauge my effectiveness as a coach because I want to provide the kind of support you need to be successful. Please help me in meeting this goal.

Using the following scale, with 1 being not confident, 3 being somewhat confident, and 5 indicating very confident, how confident are you in your ability to do the following as it relates to teaching with clarity?

"I know where I'm going." I understand my current performance and how it relates to my professional growth.	 Please elaborate:
"I have the tools for the journey." I understand that I can select from a range of strategies to move my learning forward, especially when progress is interrupted.	 Please elaborate:
"I monitor my progress." I seek and respond to feedback from others to assess my own performance. I know that making mistakes is expected and indicates an opportunity for further learning.	 Please elaborate:

(Continued)

(Continued)

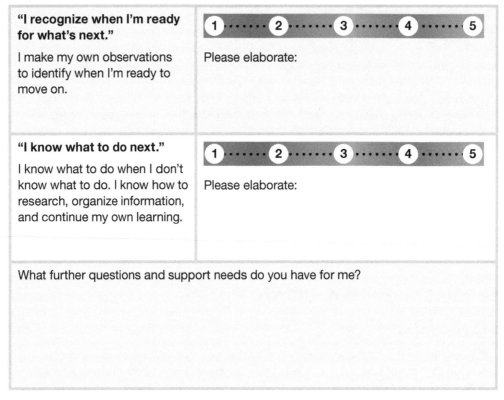

"I recognize when I'm ready for what's next." I make my own observations to identify when I'm ready to move on.	1 ···· 2 ···· 3 ···· 4 ···· 5 Please elaborate:
"I know what to do next." I know what to do when I don't know what to do. I know how to research, organize information, and continue my own learning.	1 ···· 2 ···· 3 ···· 4 ···· 5 Please elaborate:
What further questions and support needs do you have for me?	

Source: Fisher et al. (2020, p. 21).

Tying It Together With Trust

Recall the five facets of trustworthiness in leaders (benevolence, reliability, competence, honesty, and openness) from page 34. Consider taking a moment to pause and reflect on your behaviors and interactions with your staff during the past month:

- In what ways did you develop trust specifically with new teachers?

- Were there any instances in which you unintentionally acted in a way that might have resulted in lowering their trust?

- As we move into the next month, what will you continue doing? What will you start doing? What will you stop doing?

Trust Recalibration

Looking Back to Move Forward

	EVIDENCE OF TRUSTING BEHAVIORS	EVIDENCE OF DISTRUSTING BEHAVIORS	HOW WILL I MAINTAIN OR DEVELOP TRUST NEXT MONTH?
(1) Benevolence			
(2) Reliability			
(3) Competence			
(4) Honesty			
(5) Openness			

Conclusion

In this cycle, we looked at teacher clarity and made a case for why instructional leaders, coaches, and mentors revisit learning intentions, relevance, and success criteria with their staff each year. Teaching with clarity sets the stage for fostering student ownership of their learning, which is a focus of the next cycle.

Additional Resources

For Leaders and Coaches

Fisher, D., Frey, N., Amador, O., & Assof, J. (2018). *The teacher clarity playbook, grades K–12.* Corwin.

A 7-Minute Read for New Teachers

Fisher, D., & Frey, N. (2020, June 5). 5 tips for increasing clarity in the mathematics classroom. *Corwin Connect.* https://corwin-connect.com/2020/06/5-tips-for-increasing-clarity-in-the-mathematics-classroom/?utm_source=rss&utm_medium=rss&utm_campaign=5-tips-for-increasing-clarity-in-the-mathematics-classroom

A 9-Minute Video for Expert Teachers

Fisher, D., & Frey, N. (2021, November 9). How to implement learning intentions and success criteria in the classroom. *Fisher and Frey YouTube Channel.* https://youtu.be/xqBdPjSE--g

Visit the companion website at
https://qrs.ly/9mesfwe
for additional resources.

CYCLE 5

HOW ARE WE USING EVIDENCE-BASED INSTRUCTION TO FOSTER STUDENT OWNERSHIP OF THEIR LEARNING?

(4 WEEKS)

In This Section

- **Teaching Students About Engagement**

- **Evidence-Based Instructional Practices**

Context About the Theme of Student Ownership of Learning

Newer research and wise practice indicate that intentional teaching to students about engagement can deliver results because it empowers them to own their learning (Fisher, Frey, Ortega, & Hattie, 2023). More pointedly, the focus is increasingly on teaching students about cognitive self-regulation in order to accelerate their learning. Rather than low-level compliance, informed educators seek to leverage students' ownership of learning. In other words, engagement is seen as a catalyst for learning, not an outcome. Skilled teachers can identify and replicate processes that are likely to spark student engagement, but there are limits to this approach. Extend new teachers' efforts about student engagement by equipping them with tools to teach their students about their role in engaging with learning.

We introduced the concept of student ownership of learning in the previous cycle on teaching with clarity, and now we want to expand your efforts in guiding new teachers. The purpose of the current cycle deepens the work on student ownership through the intentional teaching of engagement skills to students.

In addition, new teachers need an instructional framework to align their instruction. If we are to cognitively engage students in learning, we must utilize the learning sciences to ensure that instruction is effective and meaningful. Therefore, this cycle also features discussion of evidence-based practices to foster learning.

Teaching Students to Drive Their Learning

Experienced teachers understand that student engagement is nuanced, situational, and variable. In addition, they understand that prizing compliance sets a very low bar and does little to enhance learning. Most of us have experienced the unreliability of focusing on a limited set of outward behaviors: the seemingly daydreaming student who has absorbed every word, the forward-facing, pencil-poised student who is only thinking about the argument she had with a friend. Further, expert teachers know that there is a gradient of engagement and disengagement, from relatively passive to quite active. Berry's (2022) work with teachers captured these subtleties. We have enhanced the continuum of engagement she introduced to further describe the signals teachers see, and more importantly, skills that students can be taught. The continuum of engagement acknowledges passive and active forms of engagement and disengagement across a spectrum of six levels: *disrupting, avoiding, withdrawing, participating, investing*, and *driving* (see Figure 5.1). We have further expanded this model to include two features for students to use and one for the teacher to use:

 ▶ For students: How am I engaging with the activity?

 ▶ For students: How am I engaging with peers?

 ▶ For the teacher: What are my goals for this interaction?

Students at the *disrupting* level on the continuum are actively disengaged and actively disrupting their learning and the learning process of their peers. Someone who is in the *avoiding* level does not disrupt the learning environment, but they may participate in off-task or counterproductive behaviors to elude the learning task or avoid class or school entirely. When students *withdraw,* they do it passively, and distract themselves but not at the expense of others. Those who *participate* in the learning can still be passive; however, they engage for compliance purposes but with minimal cognitive effort. Students who *invest* in their learning take responsibility for their learning because they value it. They are curious, excited, ask questions, and collaborate with their peers. And when our students *drive,* they exhibit an active commitment to themselves as learners, set learning goals for themselves, and monitor their own progress.

Figure 5.1   Engaging in the Activity and Engaging With Peers

Active ← ——————————————————— Passive ——————————————————— → Active

	DISRUPTING	AVOIDING	WITHDRAWING	PARTICIPATING	INVESTING	DRIVING
Engaging in the Activity	Distracting others Disrupting the learning	Looking for ways to avoid work Off-task behavior	Being distracted Physically separating from group	Doing work Paying attention Responding to questions	Asking questions Feeling like what you are learning is important	Setting goals Seeking feedback Self-assessing and monitoring progress
Engaging With Peers	Arguing with peers Trying to distract	Looking busy to avoid work Finding reasons to leave the group	Sitting with the group but interacting with the group	Working with others when directed to do so	Sharing ideas and thinking with peers Following shared interests	Collaborating with others toward a shared goal Challenging each other to drive improvement
	What goals might the teacher have for engagement in the learning experience?			*I want them to follow my lead and complete certain tasks.*	*I want them to be interested in learning and actively involved in the process.*	*I want them to be proactive and collaborative learners.*
	Disengagement			**Engagement**		

Source: Adapted from Berry (2022).

Most students want to do well in school. They are motivated to do so, especially through their family's love and concern. But many don't know *how* to do well. Without instruction on how to do so, they instead come to believe that it is all about "doing school" (Jackson, 1968). Note the date of the reference: This is a decades-long problem.

What is crucial is teaching students about their engagement and providing them with lots of opportunities to self-assess their investment in their own learning every day. It gives teachers an opportunity to have a shared understanding and common language but more importantly, it invites students to participate and take ownership in their own engagement and learning journey. We have witnessed

> Kindergarten teachers using tokens so that their young students can place a marker on the portion of the continuum that reflects their goal for the day

> Third-grade teachers using a sheet protector with the continuum on every student's desk so that students can check off their self-assessment using a dry-erase marker

> Seventh-grade students setting their intention by talking with a partner at the beginning of each lesson about their goal

> Tenth-grade students using a digital exit ticket to answer a content question and then indicate their level of engagement in the lesson

In the New Teacher section of the cycle, we have a video of a high school teacher in action, teaching his own students about the continuum.

Evidence-Based Instruction

While the learning intentions and success criteria frame the learning, the lessons themselves need to provide meaningful learning experiences; that is, they adhere to the principles of the learning sciences. However, novice teachers, even though they have received training in lesson design, may have difficulty recognizing when these principles are in play. As a school leader, you have two goals for them: (1) teach using evidence-based practices that move learning forward and (2) develop their expert noticing skills. König et al. (2022) performed a systematic review of the research on expert noticing and reported that this skill is associated with responding and decision making, as well as more accurate perceptions of student learning and student work. The learning walks you conduct with the new teachers at your site can support the development of expert noticing, but only if there is a framework that defines quality instruction. That's where a coherent instructional framework pays off, as it links learning theory to the teacher's instructional moves and a growing ability to notice.

The gradual release of responsibility instructional framework accomplishes the goals of grounding instruction in evidence-based practices while honing the expert noticing of teachers (Fisher & Frey, 2021). Each of these instructional moves should occur during every lesson. It certainly does not need to be done in this order (we have never written that or said that), but the learning sciences are clear on this: students need opportunities to utilize the content, not just listen to someone else explaining it.

Focused Instruction: *What input do students need from teachers?*
Direct instruction, modeling, and worked examples are important, as is the framing of the learning intentions, relevance, and success criteria of

the lesson. Be careful that direct instruction doesn't devolve into lecture (which is not the same as direct instruction). Lectures have an effect size of −0.26, meaning they can actually reverse learning (Hattie, 2023). They are barely effective for surface-level knowledge and especially bad for deepening knowledge.

Collaborative Learning: *How will students learn from each other? How will the teacher hold students accountable for their collaborative learning?* Meaningful peer interaction is essential, and with an effect size of 0.45, collaborative learning has the potential to accelerate learning (Hattie, 2023).

Guided Instruction: *How will students receive scaffolded instruction?* Scaffolding involves the use of robust questions, prompts, and cues to address the cognitive gap between what a student can do alone and what they can accomplish with someone with more expertise (Frey & Fisher, 2010). Scaffolded instruction holds particular promise, with an effect size of 0.52 (Hattie, 2023).

Independent Learning: *How will students practice and apply what they have learned?* Practice should be deliberate and spaced to ensure long-term learning. By deliberate practice, we mean that which is hard (not impossible or unknown) and allows for feedback and guidance from an expert. Novice teachers may confuse this with homework, which should be practice of content that has already been learned, not just taught. Too often, teachers assign homework because they ran out of time during the lesson. What they really should be assigning are tasks that offer spaced practice (effect size of 0.59) and that allow for rehearsal and memorization when surface learning is still happening (0.71), both with a higher-than-average potential to accelerate learning (Hattie, 2023).

In Their Shoes

Teaching Students About Owning Their Learning Leader Reflection

Directions: Instructional leaders, coaches, and mentors are effective not only because they bring a wealth of knowledge and experience to their role but also because they connect with their coachees' reality and recall how they felt when they were in the same position.

Since it may have been a few years since you were a first-year teacher, let's take a step back to remember and put ourselves in their shoes.

(Continued)

(Continued)

1. As a new classroom teacher, was student ownership of learning, as you understand it now, an area of strength? How do you know?

_____

_____

_____

_____

_____

2. In which way was it the most challenging? Why?

_____

_____

_____

_____

3. How did you develop your area of growth? What strategies did you use to improve student cognitive engagement in your classroom?

_____

_____

_____

_____

4. Looking back, what coaching support did you receive? What do you wish you would have received?

_____

_____

_____

_____

5. How will you incorporate your experience when developing your instructional coaching plan? How will you meet the needs of new teachers?

_____

_____

_____

_____

_____

_____

Coaching Scenario for Leaders
Coach Amalia

Directions: Read the scenario below and consider what you would do if you were in Amalia's position. Then answer the follow-up questions below.

Amalia is an instructional coach at a middle school. She works with the entire staff and schedules regular classroom visits with all teachers but makes a point to observe new teachers at least twice a month. Since she only has two weeks in December to get into classrooms before winter break, Amalia wants to visit all five of the new teachers so they don't feel forgotten or left behind.

Amalia noticed an immediate pattern: four out of five of the teachers were showing movies or having holiday parties.

Follow-Up Questions

1. If you were Amalia, what initial thoughts and wonderings come to mind after finishing the walkthroughs?

_____

_____

_____

_____

_____

(Continued)

(Continued)

2. How would you prepare for the post-observation conversations with the four new teachers?

_____

_____

_____

_____

_____

3. How do you address the importance of student ownership of learning? What questions would you prepare to ask?

_____

_____

_____

_____

_____

4. What resources or options could replace "movie time" or "Fun Fridays"?

_____

_____

_____

_____

_____

Leaders Get Clear and Anticipate

With a strong onboarding process, instructional leaders and coaches send a clear message to new teachers about "how we do things." They communicate and reiterate the site's expectations around student engagement. This minimizes ambiguity so new teachers adapt and adopt best practices more quickly than if they were to navigate this theme on their own.

In Our Shoes
Student Engagement and Evidence-Based
Instruction Leader Reflection

Directions: Instructional leaders/coaches should pause first to get clear about their expectations for engagement and instruction. Then they can craft their message and provide onboarded teachers with appropriate feedback to elevate their practice.

1. Which active engagement strategies have teachers learned or shared in the past?

    _____

    _____

    _____

    _____

    _____

2. Does the site have agreements about what evidence-based instruction is? What are the components?

    _____

    _____

    _____

    _____

    _____

3. What unique challenges do you anticipate new teachers will encounter when designing instruction using evidence-based practices?

    _____

    _____

    _____

    _____

    _____

(Continued)

(Continued)

4. How will you customize your supports for each of the new teachers?

_____

_____

_____

_____

_____

Leaders Get Clear and Communicate

Now that you have a clear vision of this month's focus and what that looks like at your site, it is important to communicate this message along with your expectations. Below you will find a sample of an onboarding checklist with a suggested timeline for three groups of deliverables: Leader/Coach, New Teacher, and Together.

Onboarding Checklist

	LEADER/COACH	NEW TEACHER	TOGETHER
Week 1	Send a reminder email to new teachers about the upcoming monthly onboarding check-in meeting.	Complete the New Teachers Get Familiar and Implement interactions.	
	Put a note of appreciation in new teachers' office mailboxes. A handwritten note addressed to the new teacher will light up their day!		
	Complete the Context About the Theme section, including the interactions.		
	Complete the Leaders Get Clear and Anticipate section, including the interactions.		
	Review the Cycle 5 learning guide and slide deck at the companion website and make modifications as needed.		

	LEADER/COACH	NEW TEACHER	TOGETHER
	Invite expert teachers to join the onboarding meeting and share their best practices with new teachers. Ask them if they would welcome new teachers to visit their classrooms and ask for their availability.		
	Facilitate the monthly onboarding check-in meeting. This meeting is short (up to 30 minutes), and might occur before school, at lunch, or after school. We have provided a slide presentation for you to use and customize. Bring water and healthy snacks as tokens of appreciation.	Schedule time to visit an expert teacher's room. Complete the pre-work on the New Teachers Learn From Expert Teachers interactive feature.	Attend the monthly onboarding check-in meeting.
		Visit the expert teacher's classroom. Use the New Teachers Learn From Expert Teachers interactive feature to document your learning. Thank the expert teacher in person or by email for inviting you into their classroom.	Schedule classroom observation focused on the theme. Agree on a data collection tool. Schedule post-observation meeting.
Week 2	Send a thank-you email to new teachers for attending the onboarding meeting. Confirm the dates for observation and post-observation meetings via calendar invites. Send a thank-you email to the expert teachers who attended the onboarding meeting and invite new teachers to visit their classrooms.		
Week 3	Review the New Teachers Get Familiar and Implement section, including interactions.		Conduct classroom observation. Hold the post-observation meeting with a debrief tool.

(Continued)

(Continued)

	LEADER/COACH	NEW TEACHER	TOGETHER
Week 4	Give them an end-of-the-month token of appreciation to congratulate them on successfully completing another month.	Complete the Check-In and Follow-Up tools for interactions.	
	Review and reflect on responses from submitted Leaders Ask "How Did We Do?" surveys.		
	Complete the Trust Recalibration interaction.		
	Send a reminder email about next month's onboarding meeting (date, time, location). Include calendar invites.		

Email to New Teachers on the First Day of Cycle

(Example)

Hello _____,

I appreciate the way that you have gotten to know your students in meaningful ways. It's true that some students still try to test your nerves, and I can see how you continue to be their biggest advocate.

At our next onboarding meeting (_____), we will come together to revisit student engagement and discuss what it means to use evidence-based instructional practices. We will have expert teachers in the room who will share what they do (and don't do) and offer days and times for you to come see the magic happen in real time.

I'm looking forward to seeing you on the _____. Until then, I'm here to help so don't hesitate to reach out!

Sincerely,

_____

(Other Conversations to Consider)

- District and schoolwide committee meetings
- District and schoolwide professional development opportunities
- Local and community events
- Staff socials and events
- Student events:
  - Theater performances
  - Chorus concerts
  - Band and orchestra concerts
  - Dance competitions
  - Athletic events, games, tournaments
  - School fundraisers
  - School dances

Interactive Feature for Leaders

Invitational Email to Expert Teachers

(Example)

Hello _____,

Thank you for attending our onboarding meeting last month. I had several new teachers tell me how much they learned from you and they hoped you would come again so . . .

Our next onboarding meeting is on _____, and our new theme is student engagement and evidence-based instructional practices. I have attached a summary of this cycle's theme [attach the Context About the Theme found at the beginning of this cycle]. Are you available to join us again to share your expertise along with the days/times that you're available for them to watch the magic happen?

Thank you for making a positive impact on the next generation of educators!

Sincerely,

_____

Leaders Express Appreciation

Here is a checklist of ways that leaders/coaches can show a token of their appreciation to new teachers for all of their hard work. This could also show your teachers how to pay it forward. Showing them graciousness will move them to show and connect with their students. We recommend that you do one item from this checklist this month to make them feel welcome and a part of the school.

(Examples)

Write a one- or two-sentence message on a thank-you card. Put it in their office mailbox with a special treat:

[School or district swag]

- Lanyards
- T-shirts or sweaters from student council or ASB
- Accessories like scarves, hats, socks, etc.
- Pencils, mugs, tumblers, etc. with the school or district logo

Expert Tip: Check if there are forgotten items from previous years in the site or district supply rooms.

[Items they may need in their classrooms]

- Tissue
- Pencils or pens
- Paper
- Wipes
- Whiteboard markers
- Smelly markers
- Composition notebooks
- Gift baskets of supplies

Expert Tip: Ask parent/family groups, community members, or local businesses for donations.

[Other gift ideas]

- Gently used novels
- Reusable shopping bags or canvas tote bags
- Boxed thank-you cards

New Teachers Get Familiar and Implement

Video Reflection
Teach Students About Their Engagement

Directions: Let's look at a high school teacher as he teaches his students about their own engagement. He uses the continuum of engagement as a visual to support their learning. Do not be distracted by his content or grade level. You are developing your expert noticing. After watching Video 5.1 (available at the companion website), answer each question below.

1. How does the teacher introduce the engagement continuum? How does he make it relevant for them?

_____

_____

_____

_____

_____

2. The teacher uses a jigsaw method so that his students learn and are taught each section of the continuum. What organizational methods does he use to ensure this instructional routine runs smoothly?

_____

_____

_____

_____

_____

3. What changes in student learning took place from the beginning of the lesson until the end?

_____

_____

_____

_____

_____

(Continued)

(Continued)

4. Use what you know: In what ways did the teacher exhibit behaviors of an intentionally inviting educator?

_____

_____

_____

_____

_____

New Teachers Self-Assess
Engagement Through Student Ownership and Evidence-Based Instructional Practices

Directions: Take a moment to tap into your prior knowledge and assess yourself in the areas of a student engagement continuum and in your use of evidence-based instructional practices.

1. What successful actions have you taken to strengthen student engagement since the start of the school year? Why do you believe they have been successful?

_____

_____

_____

_____

2. Reflect on this week's learning experiences. From your observation, where do they rate on the Continuum of Engagement? Provide examples.

_____

_____

_____

_____

_____

3. What student signals do you watch for to know when you should pause to model your thinking?

_____

_____

_____

_____

_____

4. What adjustments did you make "in the moment" to reinvest students in their engagement during the lesson?

_____

_____

_____

_____

5. Looking back, were there any missed opportunities? What will you do differently as a result?

_____

_____

_____

_____

Your Turn

Practice Driving Learning Through Engagement

Directions: The continuum of engagement builds on the work we did earlier this school year on student engagement. But in order for students to move to higher levels of engagement, they must be given opportunities to do so. How can you leverage curricular decisions and instructional moves to foster student participation, investment, and especially a drive to learn?

	CURRICULUM OR CONTENT	INSTRUCTION OR PEDAGOGY
Participating in Learning • Doing work • Paying attention • Responding to questions • Observing teachers doing work • Following teacher instructions • Complying with a new rule		
Investing in Learning • Asking questions • Valuing the learning • Recognizing that there are things worth learning • Collaborating with peers • Talking about their learning with others • Thinking along with their teachers		
Driving Learning • Setting goals for themselves based on what the class is learning • Seeking feedback from others • Self-assessing and monitoring progress • Teaching others • Being inspired to learn more about a topic or pursue an interest		

New Teachers Get Familiar and Implement

Video Reflection
Use Evidence-Based Instructional Practices

Directions: Let's look at a second-grade teacher as she teaches a lesson on geometric figures. This is not new content for these students. Her goal is to have them apply what her students have been learning. Do not be distracted by her content or grade level. You are developing your expert noticing. Look for each phase of the gradual release of responsibility. After watching Video 5.2 (available at the companion website), answer each question below.

1. What is the teacher's purpose (learning intention)?

_____

_____

_____

_____

_____

2. What is the teacher modeling? How does it align with her stated purpose?

_____

_____

_____

_____

3. When do you see evidence of her guided instruction? Capture examples of questions, prompts, or cues she uses.

_____

_____

_____

_____

_____

(Continued)

(Continued)

4. The teacher provides a multilingual learner with more opportunities to practice. Why are practice and repetition useful for language learners?

_____

_____

_____

_____

_____

5. Use what you know: The teacher used Numbered Heads Together (Kagan et al., 1997) to organize her collaborative learning. Her students had used the routine many times before. What are the advantages of teaching and utilizing high-frequency routines?

_____

_____

_____

_____

_____

Your Turn

Practice Evidence-Based Instructional Practices

Directions: Choose a lesson plan that you will implement this week. Use this interactive feature to create a plan using evidence-based instructional practices framed by learning intentions, relevance, and success criteria.

What is my learning intention?	
What success criteria do I have for this lesson?	

HOW WILL I ESTABLISH RELEVANCE . . .	EVIDENCE IN LESSON DESIGN	
	TEACHER-LED	**STUDENT-LED**
1. Outside of the classroom?		
2. Co-constructed with students?		
3. Based on learning about oneself as a learner?		
4. Within the discipline?		

ACCESS POINTS	EVIDENCE IN LESSON DESIGN	
	TEACHER-LED	**STUDENT-LED**
A. Teacher modeling?		
B. Guided instruction (with questions, prompts, cues, or direct explanations)?		
C. Collaborative learning?		
D. Independent learning?		

Check-In and Follow-Up Tools for Leaders

Host capacity-building learning walks with new teachers during this cycle to help them notice how experienced teachers create intentional opportunities to foster their students' abilities to own and drive their learning. Volunteer teachers open up their classrooms for short, pre-arranged observations (about 10 minutes) for a pre-determined area of focus, in this case, opportunities for students to invest and drive their learning. An administrator, coach, or mentor can host the learning walk. The observers debrief after three classroom visits, and the discussion is confined to patterns gleaned, not about individual classrooms. The composition of the team rotates so that observers have the experience of collecting data across all three sources (teacher, students, and environment). The team debrief of the experience is conducted at the end to draw conclusions.

New teachers may not fully understand the difference between observing for patterns and evaluation. Discourage them from using evaluative statements (e.g., "I liked the way . . ." or "The teacher should have . . ."). Instead, remind them to use objective statements (e.g., "Three students described . . ." or "Two of the three classrooms provided time for students to ask questions"). In addition, remind them of the focus: student ownership of learning. Don't get distracted by the other things that might be occurring!

Classroom Learning Walk Focus

How do teachers use curriculum and instruction to foster student ownership of their learning? How does the environment support these efforts?

EXAMPLES OF INVESTING IN THEIR LEARNING	EXAMPLES OF DRIVING THEIR LEARNING
Asking questions	Setting goals for themselves based on what the class is learning
Valuing the learning	Seeking feedback from others
Recognizing that there are things worth learning	Self-assessing and monitoring progress
Collaborating with peers	Teaching others
Talking about their learning with others	Being inspired to learn more about a topic or pursue an interest
Thinking along with their teachers	

Classroom 1 Evidence

Instructional Moves to foster student ownership of learning:

Curricular Decisions to foster student ownership of learning:

Room Environment Supports:

EXAMPLES OF INVESTING IN THEIR LEARNING	EXAMPLES OF DRIVING THEIR LEARNING
Classroom 2 Evidence Instructional Moves to foster student ownership of learning: Curricular Decisions to foster student ownership of learning: Room Environment Supports:	
Classroom 3 Evidence Instructional Moves to foster student ownership of learning: Curricular Decisions to foster student ownership of learning: Room Environment Supports:	

Debrief on Patterns After Three Classrooms

	HOW DID TEACHERS USE CURRICULUM TO FOSTER STUDENT OWNERSHIP OF LEARNING?	WHAT INSTRUCTIONAL MOVES DID WE WITNESS TO FOSTER STUDENT OWNERSHIP OF LEARNING?	HOW DID THE ROOM ENVIRONMENT SUPPORT STUDENT OWNERSHIP OF LEARNING?
Emerging Patterns and Trends			

(Continued)

(Continued)

	HOW DID TEACHERS USE CURRICULUM TO FOSTER STUDENT OWNERSHIP OF LEARNING?	WHAT INSTRUCTIONAL MOVES DID WE WITNESS TO FOSTER STUDENT OWNERSHIP OF LEARNING?	HOW DID THE ROOM ENVIRONMENT SUPPORT STUDENT OWNERSHIP OF LEARNING?
What conclusions can be drawn for use in our own classrooms?			
What growth opportunities can we identify for ourselves?			
In what ways was this process helpful or not helpful? How can I better support you?			

Source: Adapted from Fisher et al. (2019, pp. 90–92).

Classroom Observation Tool

Evidence-Based Instructional Practices

Learning Intention	
Success Criteria	

RELEVANCE . . .	YES	NO	EVIDENCE
1. Outside of the classroom?			
2. Co-constructed with students?			
3. Based on learning about oneself as a learner?			
4. Within the discipline?			

ACCESS POINTS	YES	NO	EVIDENCE
A. Teacher modeling			
B. Guided instruction (with questions, prompts, cues, or direct explanations)			
C. Collaborative learning			
D. Independent learning			

Post-Observation Debrief

Evidence-Based Instructional Practices

Learning Intention	
Success Criteria	

	RELEVANCE	ACCESS POINTS
Emerging Patterns and Trends		

(Continued)

(Continued)

	RELEVANCE	ACCESS POINTS
What was your intention when . . . ?		
Was there anything that surprised you? Why?		
What is the most important thing for you to pay attention to in yourself (emotion, mindset, beliefs about students, physical presence, etc.)?		
What supports or resources might help you in your professional growth?		

New teachers are eager to collaborate with colleagues, so the onboarding process offers them opportunities to do this. One of the ways that they can develop professionally is by working with expert teachers and visiting their classrooms. Instructional leaders and coaches play a pivotal role in connecting them to mentor teachers who add to their collegial network.

New Teachers Learn From Expert Teachers

Evidence-Based Instructional Practices

Directions: You have an amazing opportunity to collaborate with and visit an expert teacher on your site. This tool is designed to ensure that you have a learning experience that will directly impact your practice with your students.

Pre-Visit Preparation

Before visiting the classroom, what are three questions that you want to ask the expert teacher related to how the teacher uses evidence-based instructional practices? Capture their responses.

QUESTIONS	ANSWERS

Look-Fors During the Visit

What three things are you looking for or hoping to see? Document evidence of those look-fors below.

LOOK-FORS EVIDENCE-BASED INSTRUCTIONAL PRACTICES	EVIDENCE

Post-Observation Reflection

Reflect on the visit to the expert teacher's classroom. Answer each question below.

1. How will this observation support your growth as a new and effective teacher?

(Continued)

2. What specific strategies or tools will you take back to your classroom?
3. Do you have any follow-up questions that you would like to ask the expert teacher?
Expert Tip: Send the expert teacher a thank-you email and include what you enjoyed about their classroom and how visiting them made you a better teacher!

New teachers need and appreciate low-stakes timely feedback. Arrange a short visit with the new teacher (10 to 15 minutes) and provide information about what you saw and heard and what questions you have to continue the conversation. This check-in tool is not a formal observation. Rather, it is a means to monitor learning and development related to evidence-based instructional practices.

Leaders Cycle Back With New Teachers

Thank you for your tireless commitment to our students! As we move forward through our progressions, it is important to revisit what we learned previously so we don't forget and continue to grow in those areas.
Directions: Read the list of previous themes. Select one and answer the questions below.
Previous Theme(s) • Setting up the physical classroom, routines, and procedures • Student engagement and classroom management • Teacher credibility, teacher expectations, and family communication • Teacher clarity (learning intentions, relevance, and success criteria)
1. What new takeaways or aha moments did you encounter? What new understandings have you reached this month about the theme you selected?
2. In what ways have you developed professionally in this area?

3. What lingering questions or wonderings do you have for a leader, coach, or expert teacher?

Leaders Ask "How Did We Do?"

Student Ownership of Learning and Evidence-Based Practices

It is very important for me to gauge my effectiveness as a coach because I want to provide evidence-based practices for onboarding new teachers. Please help me in meeting this goal.

Using the following scale, with 1 being not confident, 3 being somewhat confident, and 5 indicating very confident, how confident are you in your ability to do the following as it relates to student ownership of learning and the use of evidence-based instructional practices?

"I know where I'm going." I understand my current performance and how it relates to my professional growth.	1 ···· 2 ···· 3 ···· 4 ···· 5 Please elaborate:
"I have the tools for the journey." I understand that I can select from a range of strategies to move my learning forward, especially when progress is interrupted.	1 ···· 2 ···· 3 ···· 4 ···· 5 Please elaborate:
"I monitor my progress." I seek and respond to feedback from others to assess my own performance. I know that making mistakes is expected and indicates an opportunity for further learning.	1 ···· 2 ···· 3 ···· 4 ···· 5 Please elaborate:
"I recognize when I'm ready for what's next." I make my own observations to identify when I'm ready to move on.	1 ···· 2 ···· 3 ···· 4 ···· 5 Please elaborate:

(Continued)

(Continued)

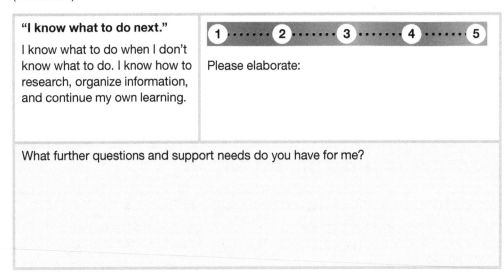

"I know what to do next."

I know what to do when I don't know what to do. I know how to research, organize information, and continue my own learning.

Please elaborate:

What further questions and support needs do you have for me?

Tying It Together With Trust

Recall the five facets of trustworthiness in leaders (benevolence, reliability, competence, honesty, and openness) from page 34. Consider taking a moment to pause and reflect on your behaviors and interactions with your staff at this crucial start of the school year:

▶ In what ways did you develop trust specifically with new teachers?

▶ Were there any instances in which you unintentionally acted in a way that might have resulted in lowering their trust?

▶ As we move into the next month, what will you continue doing? What will you start doing? What will you stop doing?

Trust Recalibration

Looking Back to Move Forward

	EVIDENCE OF TRUSTING BEHAVIORS	EVIDENCE OF DISTRUSTING BEHAVIORS	HOW WILL I MAINTAIN OR DEVELOP TRUST NEXT MONTH?
(1) Benevolence			
(2) Reliability			
(3) Competence			
(4) Honesty			
(5) Openness			

Conclusion

Student ownership of learning plays an important role in accelerating learning. It also interrupts the thinking of new teachers, who may inaccurately believe that engagement is limited to classroom management. Student ownership of learning does not happen by luck or chance. It is the direct result of deliberate choices that teachers make when designing their curriculum and instruction. Every instructional minute is valuable and is allocated to serve a clear purpose. It is important for new teachers to be aware of this connection and make thoughtful choices on behalf of their learners.

Additional Resources

For Leaders and Coaches

Fisher, D., Frey, N., Ortega, S., & Hattie, J. (2023). *Teaching students to drive their learning: A playbook on engagement and self-regulation, K–12.* Corwin.

A 4-Minute Read for New Teachers

Mosby, A., & Hamilton, S. (2022, September 14). The role of cognition in the gradual release of responsibility model. *Edutopia.* https://www.edutopia.org/article/role-cognition-gradual-release-responsibility-model/

A 45-Minute Webinar for Expert Teachers

Corwin. (2021, September 14). John Almarode and Nancy Frey: A look at how learning works. *Corwin YouTube Channel.* https://youtu.be/GouaXTmCZXk

Visit the companion website at
https://qrs.ly/9mesfwe
for additional resources.

CYCLE 6

HOW DO WE TEACH RESPONSIVELY?

(4 WEEKS)

In This Section

- **Monitoring Progress Through Formative Assessment**

- **Giving and Receiving Feedback**

Context About the Theme of Teaching Formatively and Using Feedback Wisely

The purpose of this cycle is to provide tools for building on evidence-based instruction through the use of formative assessment and feedback. When teachers lay a clear pathway for instruction, they increase students' chances of meeting the intended learning goals. Teaching with clarity and teaching for meaningful learning help to accomplish this. However, checking for understanding using formative assessment techniques allows teachers to capitalize on the moment and to teach more responsively. Novice teachers may include tasks to assess the learning at the end of the class period or the end of the day, but expert teachers integrate these throughout the lesson to monitor student progress and adjust their instruction and make decisions about what comes next.

Expert teachers embed assessment opportunities in each lesson for three reasons: (1) so students can process the information for themselves; (2) so teachers gain insight into how students are or are not moving through the learning process; and (3) so teachers collect data on the effectiveness of their own practice. These checks for understanding can come in many forms (like teacher questions, student responses, student questions, exit tickets, or a collaborative activity to name a few) but what they all have in common is that they are directly aligned with learning intentions and success criteria.

Feedback is a crucial dimension of a formative assessment system. Feedback provides opportunities for the teacher to respond. But feedback should not be a one-way transmission model from teacher to student. Feedback is bidirectional, meaning that feedback must be gathered from students, not just given. An overlooked element of feedback is that the only way feedback works is when there is mutual trust and mutual respect. It is the relationship that is the mediator. The evidence on feedback is strong, with an overall effect size of 0.54 (Hattie, 2023) but it is often misunderstood—it is not about feedback *given*, but rather feedback *received*. The bidirectionality of feedback links right back to the notions of invitational teaching and high-expectations teaching, the foci of earlier cycles. Teachers who fail to be intentionally inviting and who hold low expectations for some of their students risk damaging relationships that undermine feedback. When the relationship is not seen as a product, and the teacher is not perceived as being credible, their students disregard the feedback. And the teacher in turn fails to act on the feedback their students are giving to them.

Formative Assessment

We'll start with a myth-buster: There's no such thing as a "formative assessment." Assessment is assessment; when and how it is used is what matters. Teachers use assessments formatively to check for understanding, monitor progress, and make next-steps instructional decisions based on what knowledge is sticking and what isn't. Students use assessments formatively to monitor their own progress. Maybe a better term is "informative assessment."

Teachers use assessments summatively to measure competency at the end of a unit or course and to make decisions about grades and promotion. Students use assessments summatively to gauge their progress toward goals and standards.

We'll use the brilliant metaphor developed by Robert Stake to explain the difference between the two: "When the cook tastes the soup, it's formative. When the guests taste the soup, it's summative" (Miller et al., 2016).

There are a number of ways to check for understanding formatively; their value is only evidenced when this information (feedback) is used by the teacher to make informed decisions about what needs to happen next. If the assumption is, "I taught them. They didn't learn it. It's because they don't care/aren't listening/ aren't smart" then all that data gathering is wasted. (It may also be an indicator of a disinviting teacher.) It's how formative assessment is used to *inform* that matters. As Hattie and Zierer (2018) have noted, it's a mindframe. It ultimately has less to do with how you teach, and more to do with how you *think* about your teaching. Having said that, consider formative assessment opportunities in three broad categories: through dialogic instruction, writing, and practice testing (Fisher, Frey, Amador, & Assof, 2018).

Dialogic instruction is a primary channel for learning. These opportunities are replete in classrooms where students have lots of opportunities to pose questions (not just answer them). When a student poses a question, it's time to go into detective mode. "What does this young person's question tell me about what they know, don't know, or have a partial understanding of?" Teacher listening during student questions and discussions is challenging because they simultaneously must do two things—listen *to* and listen *for* information. Listening *to* a student is the act of locating identity within their utterances. In doing so, the teacher needs to consider how their insights and questions in turn illuminate who they are as an individual. At the same time, teachers need to be listening *for* the turns in the conversation that signal content understanding or misconceptions.

Check for understanding through writing, especially short writing prompts that provide a glimpse of what they know and do not know. These may come in the form of admit slips, such as a "do now" prompt at the beginning of class, and exit slips near the end of class. Admit slips and exit slips should be tied to the success criteria. One great approach for checking for understanding is to offer a mid-lesson check-in. Called the "muddiest point", students are invited to pause and write what the muddiest point has been for them in the lesson so far—in other words, what is still confusing? Angelo and Cross wrote about the technique in a classroom management book for college professors (1993); we have seen teachers use it with young children on whiteboards and with older ones using a Padlet digital bulletin board.

Practice tests are no-stakes quizzes that allow students and their teacher to see what is mastered and what is not yet known. They occur during the unit, not at the end. From the learner's standpoint, practice tests provide them with opportunities to retrieve information, an essential component of learning (Almarode et al., 2021). Further evidence is in its effect size of 0.49 (Hattie, 2023). When done with student analysis in mind, they become even more valuable. After scoring the results (but not putting them in the gradebook—this is practice!) provide students with the opportunity to analyze their performance in four categories:

▹ Easy items I got right

▹ Easy items I got wrong (*I need more practice*)

- ◗ Hard items I got right

- ◗ Hard items I got wrong (*I need more instruction*)

Be sure the teacher explains to students what the practice test is for and how it will be used by both of them. Otherwise, students might be worried about the effects of the quiz on their grade in the class.

Feedback Between the Teacher and the Student

Feedback comprises three aspects of feedback: giving, receiving, and adjusting (Almarode et al., 2022). Importantly, the giver may be the teacher or the student; the same is true of the receiver. The adjustment happens only when the feedback is acted upon by the receiver—as noted earlier, feedback is mediated by the relationship between the giver and the receiver. As well, the type of feedback that is given impacts its perceived usefulness. The three types of feedback are about the task, the process used in the task, and the self-regulation needed to drive learning (Hattie, 2023). Figure 6.1 contains examples of each.

You'll notice we also gave examples of things students say to teachers. This is feedback, either about the task, the processes they are using, or about their own identity. Student feedback isn't always pretty, but it requires listening *to* and listening *for* and then taking action to adjust instruction.

Figure 6.1 Three Levels of Feedback

TASK LEVEL	PROCESS LEVEL	SELF-REGULATION LEVEL
The most common type of feedback	Aimed at cognitive and metacognitive processes used to create the product or complete a task	Build student skills in monitoring their own learning processes
Builds surface-level knowledge	Fosters understanding of the relationship between concepts (deep learning)	Provides greater confidence to continue engaging with the task
Known as "corrective feedback" because it tells students if they are right or wrong	Reinforces learning strategies or provides clues to develop different ones	The student is willing to invest in and seek feedback
Not generalizable to learning because it is specific to the task	Error detection approaches to learn from mistakes	Impacts future learning situations when used to forward learning (not as a comment on their character)
More limited impact on future student learning, but useful when building surface-level knowledge	Impacts future learning situations because students can apply it to novel situations	

TEACHER-TO-STUDENT EXAMPLES	TEACHER-TO-STUDENT EXAMPLES	TEACHER-TO-STUDENT EXAMPLES
"You didn't cite your sources in the second paragraph. Add those sources to strengthen your claim." "You haven't met the success criteria yet because . . ." "Let's look at the exemplar and discuss the differences between it and your work."	"What was the approach you used to solve this problem?" "Are there other ways to verify your answer?" "How can you take what you learned here and apply it to other situations?"	"How do you know that you're on the right track?" "How could you strengthen this project so that you are achieving the success criteria?" "What did you learn about yourself as a learner that you didn't realize before?"
STUDENT-TO-TEACHER EXAMPLES	**STUDENT-TO-TEACHER EXAMPLES**	**STUDENT-TO-TEACHER EXAMPLES**
"I don't understand what I'm supposed to do next." "Did I do this right?"	"Like this?" "Isn't there an easier way to do this? Why do I have to do it this way?"	"This is too hard. I give up." "I'm too dumb. I'm not good at _____."

In Their Shoes

Using Formative Assessment and Feedback Leader Reflection

Directions: Instructional leaders, coaches, and mentors are not only effective because they bring a wealth of knowledge and experience to their role, but also because they connect with their coachees' reality and recall how they felt when they were in the same position.

Since it may have been a few years since you were a first-year teacher, let's take a step back to remember and put ourselves in their shoes.

1. As a new teacher, how did you check for understanding? What type of feedback did you give to help students?

_____

_____

_____

_____

_____

(Continued)

(Continued)

2. If you could go back, what would you do differently in these areas?

_____

_____

_____

_____

_____

3. How did you develop your skills in formative assessment and feedback?

_____

_____

_____

_____

_____

4. At that time, what coaching support would you have benefited from? What do you wish you would have received?

_____

_____

_____

_____

_____

5. How will you incorporate your experience when developing your instructional coaching plan? How will you meet the needs of new teachers?

_____

_____

_____

_____

_____

Coaching Scenario for Leaders

Janet

Directions: Read the scenario below and consider what you would do if you were Janet's assistant principal and instructional coach. Then answer the follow-up questions below.

On Monday morning before school, Janet pops into your office to tell you about the lesson plans that she worked on all weekend. She is excited about using evidence-based instructional practices and asks you to visit her classroom this week to see her lesson and get your feedback.

You visit her classroom on Wednesday and just as she said, the lesson is off to a great start. She communicated her learning intentions and success criteria and modeled her expert thinking with a think-aloud. Then she moved into what she called guided instruction, but Janet sat at her desk. There wasn't an assessment used formatively that you could find; students came to get individual help, which she described as "feedback." She interacted with students, but only with the ones who came to her. She did not move from her seat for the rest of the period.

Follow-Up Questions

1. As her assistant principal, what are your initial wonderings from the observation?

_____

_____

_____

_____

2. How would you address the importance of formative assessment and feedback for all students (not just the ones who initiate contact with her)?

_____

_____

_____

_____

_____

(Continued)

(Continued)

3. What coaching questions would you ask Janet at the post-observation meeting?

_____

_____

_____

_____

_____

4. What do you think should be her next steps? What additional resources and coaching could you provide?

_____

_____

_____

_____

_____

Leaders Get Clear and Anticipate

With a strong onboarding process, instructional leaders and coaches send a clear message to new teachers about "how we do things." They communicate and reiterate the site's expectations around student engagement. This minimizes ambiguity so new teachers adapt and adopt best practices more quickly than if they were to navigate this theme on their own.

In Our Shoes

Formative Assessment and Feedback Leader Reflection

Directions: Instructional leaders, coaches, and mentors should pause first to get clear about their expectations. Then they can craft their message and provide onboarded teachers with appropriate feedback to elevate their practice.

1. Has the staff received professional development for formative assessments and effective feedback?

_____

_____

_____

_____

2. What best practices do teachers utilize in their classrooms?

_____

_____

_____

_____

_____

3. What are the top three things that new teachers should know and be able to do in these areas?

_____

_____

_____

_____

_____

4. What unique challenges do you anticipate new teachers will encounter? How will you address and support them?

_____

_____

_____

_____

_____

Leaders Get Clear and Communicate

Now that you have a clear vision of this cycle's focus and what that looks like at your site, it is important to communicate this message along with your expectations. On the next page you will find a sample of an onboarding checklist with a suggested timeline for three groups of deliverables: Leader/Coach, New Teacher, and Together.

Onboarding Checklist

	LEADER/COACH	NEW TEACHER	TOGETHER
Week 1	Send a reminder email to new teachers about the upcoming monthly onboarding check-in meeting.	Complete the New Teachers Get Familiar and Implement interactions.	
	Put a note of appreciation in new teachers' office mailboxes. A handwritten note addressed to the new teacher will light up their day!		
	Complete the Context About the Theme section, including the interactions.		
	Complete the Leaders Get Clear and Anticipate section, including the interactions.		
	Review the Cycle 6 learning guide and slide deck at the companion website and make modifications as needed.		
	Invite expert teachers to join the onboarding meeting and share their best practices with new teachers. Ask them if they would welcome new teachers to visit their classrooms and ask for their availability.		
	Facilitate the monthly onboarding check-in meeting. This meeting is short (up to 30 minutes), and might occur before school, at lunch, or after school. We have provided a slide presentation for you to use and customize. Bring water and healthy snacks as tokens of appreciation.	Schedule time to visit an expert teacher's room. Complete the pre-work on the New Teachers Learn From Expert Teachers interactive feature.	Attend the monthly onboarding check-in meeting.
		Visit the expert teacher's classroom. Use the New Teachers Learn From Expert Teachers interactive feature to document your learning. Thank the expert teacher in person or by email for inviting you into their classroom.	Schedule classroom observation focused on the theme. Agree on a data collection tool. Schedule post-observation meeting.

	LEADER/COACH	NEW TEACHER	TOGETHER
Week 2	Send a thank-you email to new teachers for attending the onboarding meeting. Confirm the dates for observation and post-observation meetings via calendar invites. Send a thank-you email to the expert teachers who attended the onboarding meeting and invite new teachers to visit their classrooms.		
Week 3	Review the New Teachers Get Familiar and Implement section, including interactions.		Conduct classroom observation. Hold the post-observation meeting with a debrief tool.
Week 4	Give them an end-of-the-month token of appreciation to congratulate them on successfully completing another month.	Complete the Check-In and Follow-Up tools for interactions.	
	Review and reflect on responses from submitted Leaders Ask "How Did We Do?" surveys.		
	Complete the Trust Recalibration interaction.		
	Send a reminder email about next month's onboarding meeting (date, time, location). Include calendar invites.		

Email to New Teachers on the First Day of Cycle

(Example)

Hello _____,

I am amazed by you and everything you do to connect with your students. I see how they respond to you when I visit your classroom and they are so lucky to have you.

As a friendly reminder, our next onboarding meeting is coming up on (_____). For this check-in, we will develop a common understanding of monitoring progress and effective feedback. Several of our colleagues do these two things well, so expect to see these expert teachers!

(Continued)

(Continued)

Thank you for your commitment to do your best—I want you to know that I see it and it is paying off.

Sincerely,

_____

(Other Conversations to Consider)

- District and schoolwide committee meetings
- District and schoolwide professional development opportunities
- Local and community events
- Staff socials and events
- Student events:
  - Theater performances
  - Chorus concerts
  - Band and orchestra concerts
  - Dance competitions
  - Athletic events, games, tournaments
  - School fundraisers
  - School dances

Invitational Email to Expert Teachers

(Example)

Hello _____,

When I speak with our students, your name comes up often as their "favorite teacher." New teachers also hear about the impact you make, so I'd love for them to meet you.

Our next coaching cycle focused on formative assessment and providing effective feedback. I have attached a summary of this cycle's theme [attach the Context About the Theme found at the beginning of this cycle]. Since this is one of your many areas of strength, would you be willing to come to our next onboarding meeting on _____? I've personally seen the intentional teacher moves you use so if you are open/willing, would you be comfortable letting them see you in action?

Thank you for being an expert educator and a mentor for our new teachers to look up to.

Sincerely,

_____

Leaders Express Appreciation

Here is a checklist of ways that leaders/coaches can show a token of their appreciation to new teachers for all of their hard work. This could also show your teachers how to pay it forward. Showing them graciousness will move them to show and connect with their students. We recommend that you do one item from this checklist this month to make them feel welcome and a part of the school.

(Examples)

Write a one- or two-sentence message on a thank-you card. Put it in their office mailbox with a special treat:

[School or district swag]

- Lanyards

- T-shirts or sweaters from student council or ASB

- Accessories like scarves, hats, socks, etc.

- Pencils, mugs, tumblers, etc. with the school or district logo

Expert Tip: Check if there are forgotten items from previous years in the site or district supply rooms.

[Items they may need in their classrooms]

- Tissue
- Pencils or pens
- Paper
- Wipes
- Whiteboard markers
- Smelly markers
- Composition notebooks
- Gift baskets of supplies

Expert Tip: Ask parent/family groups, community members, or local businesses for donations.

[Other gift ideas]

- Gently used novels

- Reusable shopping bags or canvas tote bags

- Boxed thank-you cards

New Teachers Get Familiar and Implement

Video Reflection
Check for Understanding

Directions: Let's watch a ninth-grade math teacher as she uses formative assessment through practice testing to understand what her students know and don't know. Do not be distracted by her content or grade level. You are developing your expert noticing. Look for how she uses peer feedback as students explore an incorrect answer. After watching Video 6.1 (available at the companion website), answer each question below.

1. This teacher uses clickers to practice test items; you might use a different digital tool. How does the use of a polling routine contribute to her pacing?

   _____

   _____

2. When a large percentage of the class gets an item incorrect, how does she respond?

   _____

   _____

3. Why is it useful to withhold the correct answer so that students can process?

   _____

   _____

4. The teacher is using peer feedback in small groups to figure out a question. What did you notice among students who changed their answers?

   _____

   _____

5. How did the teacher use the students' feedback to respond with follow-up instruction?

   _____

   _____

New Teachers Self-Assess

Formative Assessment and Feedback

Directions: Take a moment to assess yourself in the areas of formative assessment and feedback.

1. How do you monitor student progress during the lesson? What strategies or activities do you use?

_____

_____

_____

_____

2. How many times do you check for understanding or have students check their own?

_____

_____

_____

_____

3. How do you respond when you discover an error or misconception?

_____

_____

_____

_____

_____

(Continued)

(Continued)

4. What type of feedback do you typically give students: statements or questions? Provide examples.

_____

_____

_____

_____

_____

5. How do you gather feedback from students about the lesson? How do you use student feedback?

_____

_____

_____

_____

_____

Your Turn

Practice Assessing Formatively to Offer and Gain Feedback

Directions: Identify three of your hard-to-reach students. These are the ones who are quiet and unassuming and hope to fly under your radar. These students often get less feedback and seldom offer feedback. Make a plan to initiate and get started!

NAME OF STUDENT	WHAT ASSESSMENT INFORMATION WILL YOU GATHER FORMATIVELY?	WHAT FEEDBACK WILL YOU OFFER?	WHAT FEEDBACK WILL YOU GATHER FROM THE STUDENT?

TYPES OF FEEDBACK YOU MIGHT OFFER			
NAME OF STUDENT	**TASK LEVEL?**	**PROCESS LEVEL?**	**SELF-REGULATION LEVEL?**

FEEDBACK YOU WOULD LIKE TO RECEIVE			
NAME OF STUDENT	**TASK LEVEL?**	**PROCESS LEVEL?**	**SELF-REGULATION LEVEL?**

Check-In and Follow-Up Tools for Leaders

New teachers need and appreciate low-stakes timely feedback. Arrange a short visit with the new teacher (10 to 15 minutes) and provide information about what you saw and heard and what questions you have to continue the conversation. This check-in tool is not a formal observation. Rather, it is a means to monitor learning and development related to assessment used formatively to provide feedback.

Classroom Observation Tool

Monitoring Progress and Feedback

Learning Intention	
Success Criteria	

ASSESSMENTS TO CHECK FOR UNDERSTANDING	YES	NO	EVIDENCE
Using dialogic instruction			
Checks for understanding Using writing			
Practice tests			
Other techniques			
FEEDBACK	YES	NO	EVIDENCE
Task level			
Process level			
Self-regulation level			
Teacher seeks feedback from student(s)			

Post-Observation Debrief

Assessments Used Formatively for Feedback

Learning Intention		
Success Criteria		

	ASSESSMENT USED FORMATIVELY	FEEDBACK
Emerging Patterns and Trends		
How was the lesson you planned different from the lesson you taught?		
How did you use feedback gained from your checks for understanding to shape the lesson?		
How will you use their understanding to plan future instruction?		
In what ways do you believe your assessment, used formatively paired with feedback, contributes to your teacher credibility (trust, competence, dynamism, immediacy)?		
What resources and supports might assist you in your professional learning in this area?		

New teachers are eager to collaborate with colleagues and learn more about how they think about teaching and learning. This onboarding process offers them opportunities to do this. One of the ways that they can develop professionally is by working with expert teachers and visiting their classrooms. Instructional leaders and coaches play a pivotal role in connecting them to mentor teachers who add to their collegial network.

New Teachers Learn From Expert Teachers

Formative Assessment and Feedback

Directions: You have an amazing opportunity to collaborate with and visit an expert teacher on your site. This tool is designed to ensure that you have a learning experience that will directly impact your practice with your students.

Pre-Visit Preparation

Before visiting the classroom, what are three questions that you want to ask the expert teacher related to assessment used formatively and feedback? Capture their responses below.

QUESTIONS	ANSWERS

Look-Fors During the Visit

What three elements are you looking for or hoping to see? Document evidence of those look-fors below.

LOOK-FORS (ASSESSMENTS FOR FORMATIVE USE AND FEEDBACK)	EVIDENCE

LOOK-FORS (ASSESSMENTS FOR FORMATIVE USE AND FEEDBACK)	EVIDENCE

Post-Visit Reflection

Reflect on the visit to the expert teacher's classroom. Answer each question below.

1. How will this observation support your growth as a new and effective teacher?

2. What specific strategies or tools will you take back to your classroom?

3. Do you have any follow-up questions that you would like to ask the expert teacher?

Expert Tip: Send the expert teacher a thank-you email and include what you enjoyed about their classroom and how visiting them made you a better teacher!

Leaders Cycle Back With New Teachers

Thank you for your tireless commitment to our students! As we move forward through our progressions, it is important to revisit what we learned previously so we don't forget and continue to grow in those areas.

Directions: Reflect on a previous theme of your choice and answer the questions below.

Previous Theme(s)

- Setting up the physical classroom, routines, and procedures
- Student engagement and universal classroom management
- Teacher credibility, teacher expectations, and family communication
- Teacher clarity (learning intentions, relevance, and success criteria)
- Fostering student ownership of learning and using evidence-based instructional practices

(Continued)

(Continued)

1. What new takeaways or aha moments did you encounter? What new understandings have you reached this month about the theme you selected?

2. In what ways have you continued to develop professionally in this area?

3. What lingering questions or wonderings do you have for a leader, coach, or expert teacher?

Leaders Ask "How Did We Do?"

Teaching Responsively

It is very important for me to gauge my effectiveness as a coach because I want to provide a responsive professional environment. Please help me in meeting this goal.

Using the following scale, with 1 being not confident, 3 being somewhat confident, and 5 indicating very confident, how confident are you in your ability to do the following as it relates to formative assessment and feedback?

"I know where I'm going." I understand my current performance and how it relates to my professional growth.	 Please elaborate:
"I have the tools for the journey." I understand that I can select from a range of strategies to move my learning forward, especially when progress is interrupted.	 Please elaborate:
"I monitor my progress." I seek and respond to feedback from others to assess my own performance. I know that making mistakes is expected and indicates an opportunity for further learning.	 Please elaborate:

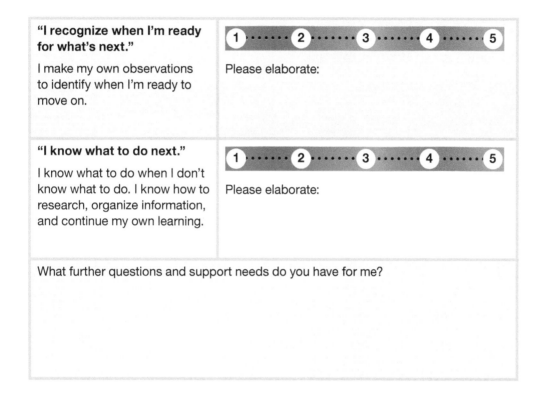

"I recognize when I'm ready for what's next."	1 ······ 2 ······ 3 ······ 4 ······ 5
I make my own observations to identify when I'm ready to move on.	Please elaborate:
"I know what to do next."	1 ······ 2 ······ 3 ······ 4 ······ 5
I know what to do when I don't know what to do. I know how to research, organize information, and continue my own learning.	Please elaborate:

What further questions and support needs do you have for me?

Tying It Together With Trust

Recall the five facets of trustworthiness in leaders (benevolence, reliability, competence, honesty, and openness) from page 34. Consider taking a moment to pause and reflect on your behaviors and interactions with your staff at this crucial start of the school year:

▸ In what ways did you develop trust specifically with new teachers?

▸ Were there any instances in which you unintentionally acted in a way that might have resulted in lowering their trust?

▸ As we move into the next month, what will you continue doing? What will you start doing? What will you stop doing?

Trust Recalibration

Looking Back to Move Forward

	EVIDENCE OF TRUSTING BEHAVIORS	EVIDENCE OF DISTRUSTING BEHAVIORS	HOW WILL I MAINTAIN OR DEVELOP TRUST NEXT MONTH?
(1) Benevolence			
(2) Reliability			
(3) Competence			
(4) Honesty			
(5) Openness			

Conclusion

"Teaching" is not synonymous with "learning." In other words, just because a new teacher designs an "effective" lesson plan on paper, we cannot actually confirm that it was effective unless we have data to reveal student learning. Teachers collect data daily by monitoring their progress through formative assessment opportunities. This includes some pre-planning to picture the indicators they expect to see and pair it with the level of feedback needed. By pairing assessment with feedback, they invest in their credibility as a teacher. Waiting until the end of the chapter or even the end of the day to check for understanding is too late. Don't leave student learning to chance. A teacher's credibility is further enhanced when they seek and utilize feedback from their students. The practice of seeking feedback scales with a teacher's perceived sense of immediacy.

Additional Resources

For Leaders and Coaches

Almarode, J., Fisher, D., & Frey, N. (2022). *How feedback works: A playbook*. Corwin.

A 10-Minute Read for New Teachers

McTighe, J. (2021, January 28). 8 quick checks for understanding. *Edutopia.* https://www.edutopia.org/article/8-quick-checks-understanding/

An 8-Minute Read for Expert Teachers

Donohoo, J., Bryen, S., & Weishar, B. (2019, June 27). A matrix of feedback for learning: A brief summary. *Corwin Connect.* https://corwin-connect.com/2019/06/a-matrix-of-feedback-for-learning-a-brief-summary/?fbclid=IwAR13WxLMZ93_tZeasN0pfFTCHw1crPb23k96lbG6Bl31MwLyLiSCrfPcSMU

Visit the companion website at
https://qrs.ly/9mesfwe
for additional resources.

CYCLE 7
HOW WILL STUDENTS KNOW THEY ARE SUCCESSFUL?
(4 WEEKS)

In This Section

- **Using Assessments Summatively to Measure Mastery of Standards**

- **Grading Practices**

Context About the Theme of Summative Assessments and Grading

Standards are the throughline for content, instruction, and assessment. Assessments are used summatively by teachers to make decisions about grades and promotion. Students use summative assessments to gauge their continued progress toward standards. Ideally, there is an overlap between a teacher's use and their students' use of these assessments. As the end of the year approaches, the results of summative assessments should also be used by the teacher to analyze the impact of teaching on student learning. In addition, curriculum maps should be reviewed to make improvements and adjustments for next year. The purpose of this cycle is to shine a spotlight on the uses of summative assessments for measurement and grading. At this time of the school year, novice teachers may view student performance as a sorting task. In other words, they might mistakenly believe that the grades they give perform as a way to sort students into two groups: "The ones who got it, and the ones who didn't." Assessments that are used for this purpose should be understood as feedback to the teacher. In addition, it is an opportunity to analyze whether there were gaps in their teaching so they can correct them for next year.

Assessment Bias

The fact is that we all like to believe that we are completely objective; the truth is we are not. As humans, we bring biases to every interaction we have because we are hard-wired to seek patterns. In fact, our ability to see patterns serves as kind of a cognitive shortcut. It serves us well in many instances because it allows us to rapidly reach conclusions (Tversky & Kahneman, 1974). There are times when these cognitive shortcuts are particularly useful, such as when you are driving. But there are other times when they can be potentially harmful. Assessment bias is one of those instances, and while we can't completely eliminate it, being aware of it can alert us as to when it is occurring.

Assessment bias happens when we interpret test results and allow ourselves to use the cognitive shortcut to reach a conclusion that is inaccurate. Greenstein (2019) identified six of them, derived from the research on the subject. Can you find yourself in any of these? We can.

> *Confirmation bias* is the search for further evidence to confirm what we already believe to be true. Viewing some assessment data that confirm a deficit, while disregarding other data that point to gains, is an example of confirmation bias.

> *Optimism bias* can happen when we dismiss a student's learning gap because we want to believe they are doing just fine. "They didn't do well on this benchmark assessment, but they'll catch up by the next one."

> *Pessimism bias* is the opposite. "I told you they wouldn't be able to master multiplication. They don't have number sense. The pandemic is to blame, and they'll be behind for their whole academic career." It's the "Chicken Little effect"—the sky is falling and there isn't anything we can do about it.

‣ *Reliance on partial information* can be especially damaging and we're all guilty of this at times. We think we know the whole story, and therefore we stop seeking out more information—for instance, a student's traumatic experience becomes the reason why they aren't doing well academically, without investigating what other gaps and strengths may exist.

‣ *Illusion of knowledge* can get the best of us. It is the belief that we know more than we actually do and an overconfidence in our decision making and a disregard for what others who are less familiar to us may know. "Never mind what the new district assessment coordinator says about the reading benchmark. I've taught fourth grade for 10 years and I know what this means."

These biases are certainly not confined exclusively to novice teachers; we are all subject to these assessment biases. However, expert teachers are on guard for these. They ask,

‣ "What else do I need to know about this child?"

‣ "What don't I know about this student?"

‣ "Is there someone else who can interpret this data differently?"

These assessment biases, left unchecked and unchallenged, feed into fallacies about grading.

Grading and Its Many Fallacies

If there is ever a time in a novice teacher's first year when they are likely to revert to their own schooling experiences (never mind current research), it is when making grading decisions. Many new teachers approach grading by applying whatever system was used when they were in school. Of course, this is a huge problem, as there has been much that has been learned about equitable grading practices and the presence of grading bias, which differs from assessment bias (Doyle et al., 2023; Griffin & Townsley, 2022).

One aspect of grading bias has to do with the intersection of vague grading standards for students of color (Quinn, 2020). The researcher asked more than 1,500 teachers to digitally score student writing using either vague grading criteria (*do you believe this student is above, at, or below grade level?*) or with specific grading criteria in the form of a rubric, a device used to communicate success criteria. He then varied the student writing they saw, which was identical except for race-signaling names (e.g., writing about a brother named Connor or Deshawn). When presented with vague grading criteria, participants scored student writing lower in the cases when Deshawn was discussed, compared to Connor. However, these grading biases disappeared when clear grading criteria were used. Yet another reason why clearly communicated success criteria work in favor of all students (Crichton & McDaid, 2016).

Grading biases are further influenced by misconceptions about the purpose of awarding grades. The outcome is that students continue to believe that grades are a "points game" that is divorced from learning. These misconceptions become barriers to grading reform efforts. Guskey (2011) noted five such barriers that serve as obstacles that continue to persist and his retort to each statement:

- **Misconception 1:** *"Grades should provide the basis for differentiating students."* Guskey asks, "Is our purpose as teachers to *select* talent, or to *develop* talent?"

- **Misconception 2:** *"Grade distributions should represent a bell-shaped curve."* He notes that random distribution only works when nothing intervenes. Learning is an intervention.

- **Misconception 3:** *"Grades should be based on students' standing among classmates."* Guskey states that standing tells us nothing about learning.

- **Misconception 4:** *"Poor grades prompt students to try harder."* The evidence is that low-achieving students withdraw further from learning.

- **Misconception 5:** *"Students should receive one grade for each subject or course."* This effort requires teachers to fold all they know about a student into a single number or letter, resulting in a hodgepodge that includes effort, compliance, behavior, and measures of learning.

The most dangerous assumption, and one that makes novice teachers especially vulnerable to adopting these misconceptions, is a pervasive attitude that communicates "We've always done it this way" (Guskey, 2011). Stagnate attitudes among experienced faculty (not we didn't say *expert*—there is a difference) perpetuate educational models that have long been understood to be problematic.

Designing Assessments for Students and for the Teacher

Add this to the stew of problems with grading for novice teachers: they have little experience in designing assessments to be used summatively, and few have ever had a formal course in measurement and evaluation during their preservice training. Again, this leaves them subject to developing ineffective assessment instruments that are more intuitive than informed (Rogers et al., 2022). An *assessment-literate teacher* means a teacher able to

- Design and select assessment instruments

- Score and interpret them knowledgeably

- Understand the limitations that each assessment possesses

- Utilize assessment to inform the learner

Novice teachers can benefit from common assessments, benchmarks, and interims that have been designed by skilled educators. In addition, the use of such assessments can buffer them against design errors they might otherwise make. Some common design errors that can be easily remedied in formative and summative assessments:

- Don't use nonsense distractors in multiple-choice questions because they do not yield any actionable feedback.

▶ Avoid ambiguously worded short answer items that can confuse students or lead them astray.

▶ Locate fill-in-the-blank items at the end of a statement, rather than in the middle.

▶ Save true-false questions for true dichotomous concepts, not trivial facts.

In addition, there should be multiple ways for students to demonstrate their learning. Summative assessments shouldn't only look like traditional tests; there should be a mixture of performance assessments, such as research projects, formal presentations, Socratic seminars, debates, or other formal discussion events should be included.

Assessments that are administered summatively should be planned so that students have an opportunity to analyze their performance and take further action. In the last cycle, we introduced using student analysis formatively in practice testing. Keep that going by giving them another opportunity after the summative assessment (see Figure 7.1).

Figure 7.1 Student Analysis of Performance

EASY ITEMS I GOT RIGHT	EASY ITEMS I GOT WRONG *(I NEED MORE PRACTICE)*
HARD ITEMS I GOT RIGHT	**HARD ITEMS I GOT WRONG** *(I NEED MORE INSTRUCTION)*

Once students analyze their results, one or more lessons are dedicated to re-teaching items identified by students as challenging items, and that they got wrong. This can be accomplished in a number of ways, including providing independent enrichment activities for other students, partnering with a colleague to trade students so that one can reteach while the other provides enrichment, or setting up a classwide peer tutoring session. Students work in groups of 3 to 5 each, and all members have the opportunity to serve as both tutors and tutees.

The students' analyses of what they found challenging and easy represent an opportunity for the teacher to compare with what they taught well, and what should be improved. In some cases, a teacher may note that they did not teach a particular skill or concept, or perhaps only taught it superficially. These assessment analyses provide teachers with feedback that can be used to make any adjustments needed to their curriculum map for next year's classes.

In Their Shoes

Summative Assessments and Grading Leader Reflection

Directions: Instructional leaders, coaches, and mentors are not only effective because they bring a wealth of knowledge and experience to their role but also because they connect with their coachees' reality and recall how they felt when they were in the same position.

Since it may have been a few years since you were a first-year teacher, let's take a step back to remember and put ourselves in their shoes.

1. As a first-year teacher, what did you use for summative assessments? Did you use one that was already created or create your own?

_____

_____

_____

_____

_____

2. What was the grading policy in your class and school? What method did you use to grade assignments and assessments?

_____

_____

_____

_____

_____

3. What do you know now, as an experienced educator, that you wish you knew back then about summative assessments and grading?

_____

_____

_____

_____

_____

4. Looking back, what coaching support did you receive? What do you wish you would have received?

_____

_____

_____

_____

_____

5. How will you incorporate your experience when developing your instructional coaching plan? How will you meet the needs of new teachers?

_____

_____

_____

_____

_____

Coaching Scenario for Leaders

Hugo

Directions: Read the scenario below and consider what you would do if you were Hugo's instructional coach. Then answer the follow-up questions below.

Your site has been doing a lot of work with common assessments. Each PLC+ team created end-of-unit assessments. Hugo received a copy of each one and while he was initially relieved that this work was "already been done for him," he now realizes that he didn't cover many of the standards and his students will not perform well on it.

Follow-Up Questions

1. Hugo's experience is a common one, especially for new teachers. What were your initial thoughts and wonderings as you read the scenario?

_____

_____

_____

_____

_____

(Continued)

(Continued)

2. What questions would you ask Hugo in your coaching session?

_____

_____

_____

_____

3. What would be your next steps as his coach? How will you help him bridge the disconnect between his instruction and the assessments?

_____

_____

_____

_____

_____

Leaders Get Clear and Anticipate

With a strong onboarding process, instructional leaders and coaches send a clear message to new teachers about "how we do things." They communicate and reiterate the site's expectations around student engagement. This minimizes ambiguity so new teachers adapt and adopt best practices more quickly than if they were to navigate this theme on their own.

In Our Shoes

Summative Assessments and Grading Leader Reflection

Directions: Instructional leaders/coaches should pause first to get clear about their expectations. Then they can craft their message and provide onboarded teachers with appropriate feedback to elevate their practice.

1. Does the site have agreed-upon expectations regarding summative assessments and/or common benchmarks?

_____

_____

_____

2. Is there a standard grading policy for your district? How do teachers set up their gradebooks?

3. What are the top three things that new teachers should know and be able to do in these areas?

4. What unique challenges do you anticipate new teachers will encounter?

5. How will you differentiate your expectations for new teachers? What resources and ongoing coaching support will you offer?

Leaders Get Clear and Communicate

Now that you have a clear vision of this cycle's focus and what that looks like at your site, it is important to communicate this message along with your expectations. Below you will find a sample of an onboarding checklist with a suggested timeline for three groups of deliverables: Leader/Coach, New Teacher, and Together.

Onboarding Checklist

	LEADER/COACH	NEW TEACHER	TOGETHER
Week 1	Send a reminder email to new teachers about the upcoming monthly onboarding check-in meeting.	Complete the New Teachers Get Familiar and Implement interactions.	
	Put a note of appreciation in new teachers' office mailboxes. A handwritten note addressed to the new teacher will light up their day!		
	Complete the Context About the Theme section, including the interactions.		
	Complete the Leaders Get Clear and Anticipate section, including the interactions.		
	Review the Cycle 7 learning guide and slide deck at the companion website and make modifications as needed.		
	Invite expert teachers to join the onboarding meeting and share their best practices with new teachers. Ask them if they would welcome new teachers to visit their classrooms and ask for their availability.		
	Facilitate the monthly onboarding check-in meeting. This meeting is short (up to 30 minutes), and might occur before school, at lunch, or after school. We have provided a slide presentation for you to use and customize. Bring water and healthy snacks as tokens of appreciation.	Schedule time to visit an expert teacher's room. Complete the pre-work on the New Teachers Learn From Expert Teachers interactive feature.	Attend the monthly onboarding check-in meeting.

	LEADER/COACH	NEW TEACHER	TOGETHER
		Visit the expert teacher's classroom. Use the New Teachers Learn From Expert Teachers interactive feature to document your learning. Thank the expert teacher in person or by email for inviting you into their classroom.	Schedule classroom observation focused on the theme. Agree on a data collection tool. Schedule post-observation meeting.
Week 2	Send a thank-you email to new teachers for attending the onboarding meeting. Confirm the dates for observation and post-observation meetings via calendar invites. Send a thank-you email to the expert teachers who attended the onboarding meeting and invite new teachers to visit their classrooms.		
Week 3	Review the New Teachers Get Familiar and Implement section, including interactions.		Conduct classroom observation. Hold the post-observation meeting with a debrief tool.
Week 4	Give them an end-of-the-month token of appreciation to congratulate them on successfully completing another month.	Complete the Check-In and Follow-Up interactions.	
	Review and reflect on responses from submitted Leaders Ask "How Did We Do?" surveys.		
	Complete the Trust Recalibration interaction.		
	Send a reminder email about next month's onboarding meeting (date, time, location). Include calendar invites.		

Email to New Teachers on the First Day of Cycle

(Example)

Hello _____,

Can you believe that the school year ends soon? Time flies when we're in the business of helping young people realize their aspirations.

We will wrap up the school year with our last onboarding cycle: summative assessments and grading. We have _____ joining us at our check-in meeting on _____ to share a few talking points in these areas. The great news is that they already agreed to open their doors, so feel free to schedule a classroom visit with them (don't forget to use the New Teachers Learn From Expert Teachers tool)!

Only the bravest, brightest, and best become teachers. You are no exception.

Sincerely,

_____

(Other Conversations to Consider)

- District and schoolwide committee meetings
- District and schoolwide professional development opportunities
- Local and community events
- Staff socials and events
- Student events:
  - Theater performances
  - Chorus concerts
  - Band and orchestra concerts
  - Dance competitions
  - Athletic events, games, tournaments
  - School fundraisers
  - School dances

Invitational Email to Expert Teachers

(Example)

Hello _____,

When I visit your classroom, I see how you intentionally design meaningful learning experiences that align with learning intentions and success criteria. Your student test scores show that what you do works.

The new teachers and I invite expert teachers like you to join us at our onboarding check-in meetings. Our last one is on _____; are you able to join us? For this cycle, we will develop common understanding and expectations about summative assessments and grading. I have attached a summary of this cycle's theme [attach the Context About the Theme found at the beginning of this cycle]. This group loves to collaborate, so I know that they'll be ready with questions and would check out what you do with your students if you're open to this.

We really hope to see you on _____—our new teachers have been asking for you to come!

Sincerely,

_____

Leaders Express Appreciation

Here is a checklist of ways that leaders/coaches can show a token of their appreciation to new teachers for all of their hard work. This could also show your teachers how to pay it forward. Showing them graciousness will move them to show and connect with their students. We recommend that you do one item from this checklist this month to make them feel welcome and a part of the school.

(Examples)

Write a one- or two-sentence message on a thank-you card. Put it in their office mailbox with a special treat:

[School or district swag]

- Lanyards

- T-shirts or sweaters from student council or ASB

- Accessories like scarves, hats, socks, etc.

- Pencils, mugs, tumblers, etc. with the school or district logo

Expert Tip: Check if there are forgotten items from previous years in the site or district supply rooms.

[Items they may need in their classrooms]

- Tissue
- Pencils or pens
- Paper
- Wipes

(Continued)

(Continued)

- Whiteboard markers
- Smelly markers
- Composition notebooks
- Gift baskets of supplies

Expert Tip: Ask parent/family groups, community members, or local businesses for donations.

[Other gift ideas]

- Gently used novels
- Reusable shopping bags or canvas tote bags
- Boxed thank-you cards

New Teachers Get Familiar and Implement

Video Reflection

Reflecting on Assessment With a Colleague

Directions: Strengthen your ability to make assessment and grading decisions by engaging in microteaching with a more experienced colleague. Watch the video of a new teacher and an experienced teaching holding a microteaching discussion about an in-class assessment of new learning. The new teacher has recorded herself and has questions about the data she gathered during her instruction. After watching Video 7.1 (available at the companion website), answer each question below.

1. The new teacher chose a portion of the video for her selected focus. What was the focus of the conversation?

   _____

   _____

2. The experienced teacher listens carefully but does not make suggestions. Instead, he poses reflective questions. What questions does he ask that are meant to spark her reflective thinking?

   _____

   _____

3. What might you advise the new teacher to consider as she prepares a summative assessment of this material?

   _____

   _____

New Teachers Self-Assess

Summative Assessments and Grading

Directions: Take a moment to assess yourself in these areas.

1. How do you design summative assessments? What principles do you consider when creating them?

   _____

   _____

   _____

   _____

2. Do your summative assessments reflect the knowledge, skills, and concepts in the standards? Why or why not?

   _____

   _____

   _____

   _____

3. What do you do after you grade summative assessments? What are students expected to do with them?

   _____

   _____

   _____

   _____

4. What is your grading policy? Does it reflect what students do or what they learn?

   _____

   _____

   _____

   _____

   _____

Your Turn

Practice Designing Summative Assessments

Directions: Get a copy of the next summative assessment you plan to use with students. Determine the extent to which it aligns with the standards and learning intentions.

ASSESSMENT FORMATS TO BE USED (CIRCLE ALL THAT APPLY)	EVIDENCE IN SUMMATIVE ASSESSMENT	
	HOW WILL IT BE ADMINISTERED?	SUPPORTING INFORMATION (CIRCLE ALL THAT APPLY)
Multiple-Choice Items	• Small group • Individual • Paper and Pencil • Computer	• Directions for Students • Scoring guide or rubric • Estimated Time for Task(s)
Dichotomous Choice Items		
Short, Constructed Response Items	Content Standards to Be Assessed:	Evidence/Items:
Extended Essay Response	Skills or Performance to be assessed:	Evidence/Items:
Culminating Individual Project	Is it visually clear and uncluttered? To be corrected:	Is it culturally relevant? To be corrected:
Culminating Group Project		
Performance	Is the readability appropriate for the grade level? To be corrected:	How will students be able to analyze their results?
Portfolio or Exhibition		
	Degree of Complexity: • Fully complex for the standards • Partially complex compared to standards • Below grade-level standards • To be corrected:	What plans do you have for follow-up teaching? What plans do you have for enrichment?

RELEVANCE	EVIDENCE IN SUMMATIVE ASSESSMENT
1. Outside of the classroom?	
2. Based on learning about oneself as a learner?	
3. Within the discipline?	

Check-In and Follow-Up Tools for Leaders

This cycle's check-in tool is somewhat different than others because it doesn't involve a classroom visit. Instead, it is a conversation with the novice teacher about summative assessment design and analysis. Host an assessment review with the new teachers in your building. Collect three good examples of assessments used by expert teachers, and make sure to remove any identifying features (name, etc.). If you don't want to use ones from your school, locate other examples from your district curriculum director, or on the Internet.

Plan for a 30- to 45-minute session with the new teachers using the assessment analysis tool below. Help teachers use criteria for being able to evaluate quality assessments.

ASSESSMENT GALLERY WALK		
Purpose of Assessment:		
Grade Level:		
Course or Subject Area:		
When was it administered? (Quarter 1, 2, 3, or 4)		
Item Type(s): Check all that apply	Supporting Information: Check all that apply	Unbiased assessments
• Multiple-choice items	• Directions for Students	• Visually clear
• Dichotomous choice items	• Scoring guide or rubric	• Somewhat cluttered
• Short, constructed response items	• Estimated Time for Task(s)	*Suggestions for improvement:*
• Extended essay response		Directions and Item construction
• Culminating individual project	Administration Check all that apply	• Readability appropriate to grade level
• Culminating group project	• Small group	• Readability is too high
• Performance	• Individual	*Suggestions for improvement:*
• Portfolio or exhibition	• Paper and Pencil	Culturally Relevant
	• Computer	Free from cultural biases
	Content Knowledge to be assessed:	May be difficult or confusing for some students
	Skills or Performance to be assessed:	*Suggestions for improvement:*
	Compared to the grade-level or course standards, are the items appropriately complex?	
	• Fully complex for the standards	
	• Partially complex compared to standards	
	• Below grade-level standards	

Post-Assessment Review Debrief

	Teacher Students Environment
Emerging Patterns and Trends	
What features stood out to us as positive considerations?	
What improvements, if any, did we recommend?	
What are the implications for your summative assessment design practices?	
In what ways was this process helpful or not helpful? How can I better support you?	

New teachers are eager to collaborate with colleagues so the onboarding process offers them opportunities to do this. One of the ways that they can develop professionally is by working with expert teachers. Leaders and coaches play a pivotal role in connecting them to mentor teachers who add to their collegial network. This experience is outside of the classroom and is accomplished through a meeting to foster discussion about summative assessments and grading.

New Teachers Learn From Expert Teachers

Summative Assessments and Grading

Directions: You have an amazing opportunity to collaborate with an expert teacher on your site. This tool is designed to ensure that you have a learning experience that will directly impact your practice with your students.

Pre-Meeting Preparation: Summative Assessments

Before you meet, what are three questions that you want to ask the expert teacher related to summative assessments? Capture their responses below.

QUESTIONS	ANSWERS

Pre-Meeting Preparation: Grading

Before you meet, what are three questions that you want to ask the expert teacher related to summative assessments? Capture their responses below.

QUESTIONS	ANSWERS

(Continued)

(Continued)

| **Post-Meeting Reflection** |
| Reflect on your discussion with the expert teacher. Answer each question below. |
| 1. How will this discussion support your growth as a new and effective teacher? |
| 2. What specific strategies or tools will you take back to your classroom? |
| 3. Do you have any follow-up questions that you would like to ask the expert teacher? |
| **Expert Tip:** Send the expert teacher a thank-you email and include what you enjoyed about their classroom and how visiting them made you a better teacher! |

Leaders Cycle Back With New Teachers

| Thank you for your tireless commitment to our students! As we move forward through our progressions, it is important to revisit what we learned previously so we don't forget and continue to grow in those areas. |
| **Directions:** Reflect on a previous theme of your choice and answer the questions below. |
| *Previous Theme(s)* |

- Setting up the physical classroom, routines, and procedures
- Student engagement and universal classroom management
- Teacher credibility, teacher expectations, and family communications
- Teacher clarity (learning intentions, relevance, and success criteria)
- Fostering student ownership of learning and using evidence-based instructional practices
- Formative assessment and feedback

| 1. What new takeaways or aha moments did you encounter? What new understandings have you reached this month about the theme you selected? |

2. In what ways have you continued to develop professionally in this area?

3. What lingering questions or wonderings do you have for a leader, coach, or expert teacher?

Leaders Ask "How Did We Do?"

Summative Assessments and Grading

It is very important for me to gauge my effectiveness as a coach because I want to provide a professional environment that invests in your growth. Please help me in meeting this goal.

Using the following scale, with 1 being not confident, 3 being somewhat confident, and 5 indicating very confident, how confident are you in your ability to do the following as it relates to summative assessments and grading?

"I know where I'm going." I understand my current performance and how it relates to my professional growth.	 Please elaborate:
"I have the tools for the journey." I understand that I can select from a range of strategies to move my learning forward, especially when progress is interrupted.	 Please elaborate:
"I monitor my progress." I seek and respond to feedback from others to assess my own performance. I know that making mistakes is expected and indicates an opportunity for further learning.	 Please elaborate:

(Continued)

(Continued)

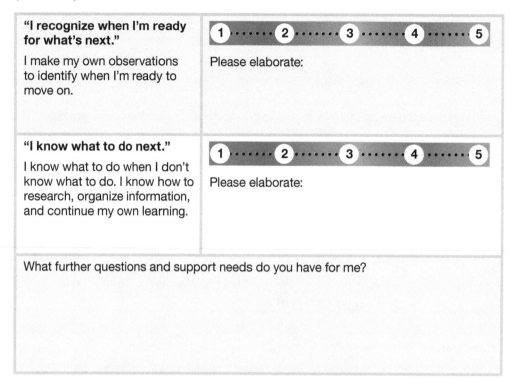

"I recognize when I'm ready for what's next." I make my own observations to identify when I'm ready to move on.	1 • • • • • 2 • • • • • 3 • • • • • 4 • • • • • 5 Please elaborate:
"I know what to do next." I know what to do when I don't know what to do. I know how to research, organize information, and continue my own learning.	1 • • • • • 2 • • • • • 3 • • • • • 4 • • • • • 5 Please elaborate:
What further questions and support needs do you have for me?	

Tying It Together With Trust

Recall the five facets of trustworthiness in leaders (benevolence, reliability, competence, honesty, and openness) from page 34. Consider taking a moment to pause and reflect on your behaviors and interactions with your staff as you close out the school year:

 ▶ In what ways did you develop trust specifically with new teachers?

 ▶ Were there any instances in which you unintentionally acted in a way that might have resulted in lowering their trust?

 ▶ As we move into the next month, what will you continue doing? What will you start doing? What will you stop doing?

Trust Recalibration

Looking Back to Move Forward

	EVIDENCE OF TRUSTING BEHAVIORS	EVIDENCE OF DISTRUSTING BEHAVIORS	HOW WILL I MAINTAIN OR DEVELOP TRUST NEXT MONTH?
(1) Benevolence			
(2) Reliability			
(3) Competence			
(4) Honesty			
(5) Openness			

Conclusion

This can be a stressful month full of mixed feelings about the assessments as well as anticipation for the end of the year. As you progress through the various assessments that each school site requires, determine what is most important with your students. Multiple indicators of learning are paramount for your assessment tool belt. To rely on one factor is limiting and may not really be a true reflection of your student's growth. The academic and emotional connections made this year with students set the stage for current progress and future success. As you move into the end of the year, continue to strive for the best for yourself while cultivating the best in others.

Additional Resources

For Leaders and Coaches

Feldman, J. C. (2018). *Grading for equity: What it is, why it matters, and how it can transform schools and classrooms.* Corwin.

A 10-Minute Read for New Teachers

Terada, Y. (2023, March 17). Why the 100-point grading scale is a stacked deck. *Edutopia.* https://www.edutopia.org/article/why-the-100-point-grading-scale-is-a-stacked-deck

A 45-Minute Video for Expert Teachers

Corwin. (2021, April 26). The game of grading with Tom Guskey: Corwin leaders coaching leaders podcast. *Corwin YouTube Channel.* https://youtu.be/u0DKzYaQQEo

---

Visit the companion website at
https://qrs.ly/9mesfwe
for additional resources.

CYCLE 8
CLOSING THE YEAR AND MOVING FORWARD
(2 WEEKS)

In This Section

- Closing the Year

- Reflecting on the Year

- Preparing for Next Year

Context About the Theme of Closing the Year and Moving Forward

It is time to celebrate our new teachers and congratulate them for successfully completing their first year! Summer break is around the corner and everyone is eager to disconnect and recharge, understandably so. However, don't succumb to the temptation to go without bringing closure to the onboarding process. As their instructional leader, instructional coach, or mentor, they need you to acknowledge how much they have grown. Their unwavering commitment and tireless effort to do right by you, their students and families, and the school community must be praised.

In addition to scheduling a celebration for new teachers (remember to invite expert teachers who also worked with them throughout the year), time should be spent revisiting the topics from the seven previous cycles. It is not uncommon to hear them describe their first year as a whirlwind, so we must reflect on our learning and check for understanding, just as we do with our students in the classroom. A collaborative discussion will provide instructional leaders and coaches with insight as they begin to think about the next set of topics for an effective Year Two onboarding process. This is also an opportunity to re-recruit both new and experienced teachers.

End the Year Strong With Students

Too often, the last few weeks of school can be a long, slow, slide into summer. Instructional minutes might be used less effectively as the message to teach with urgency is lost. New teachers are especially vulnerable to the unwritten social mores of the school. If they witness lots of movies being shown, more "Fun Fridays," and undirected time being used by students to draw, play games, or be on their devices, they are likely to do the same. This is especially true after state testing requirements are completed. It's ironic that while many educators say they "don't have enough time," the last few weeks of the school year can be marked in some places as a time when little new learning is taking place.

The final weeks of the year are an ideal time to circle back around with students to gain their reflections about their own learning. To be sure, students are looking forward to the summer break and may be getting tired of the routine of school. This is a great time to introduce curricular projects that encourage students to further explore their identities while making connections to content. A few ideas:

> **Elementary: Become an expert on something and teach the class.** Ask students to propose an idea and a how-to book (e.g., fold an origami animal, grow a plant, build a model rocket, make a paper airplane, tie knots) for your approval and make a timeline with them about how they will learn about it. Schedule one child each day to present a lesson to the class on the topic of their expertise.

> **Middle School: Use project-based learning.** Engage students in a project-based learning mini-unit on a topic related to your subject. For

instance, math students could design an adventure game, while science students could plan for a space colony to use on another planet in the solar system.

> **High School: Emphasize community service.** Young people need to consider how they can use what they know to give back to their community. English students could create books to donate to a local childcare or preschool. History students can create an assets map for a walking tour of the community that highlights local historical sites, important institutions, associations, and individuals.

Close-of-School-Year Logistics

Teachers understandably have pride of place when it comes to their classrooms. However, novice teachers may not fully understand that "their" classroom actually belongs to the school. Make sure that teachers know that their goal is to make the classroom ready to go for the next person who occupies the room. This means leaving the room as clean as possible. Think of it as turning over a rental property when the lease is done. Some schools and Human Resource departments require an administrator to sign off on the condition of the classroom as part of the requirements for obtaining their final paycheck of the year:

> Return student materials and supplies.

> Return professional materials that belong to colleagues.

> Pack up your own personal possessions.

> Return library materials.

> Declutter! Throw away items you don't need.

> Plan a clean-up afternoon and enlist the help of students to clean desks, claim belongings, and take inventory of the classroom supplies (e.g., scissors, colored pencils, protractors).

Reflect on the School Year

The final weeks of the school year should also be a time to reflect on successes, challenges, and future planning for next year. Provide new teachers with reflection questions for them to prepare in advance of a final conference with you. Here are ten possible questions:

1. What do you consider to be your greatest success this year? Why?

2. Describe your favorite day of this past school year. What happened?

3. Describe your least favorite day of the school year. What happened?

4. What student improved most this year? Why do you think they were successful?

5. What was a major challenge you faced this year?

6. What helped you to be able to address those challenges?

7. How do you believe your students would describe you?

8. Who influenced your professional practice most this year?

9. How was your communication with families?

10. If you could advise beginning-of-the-school-year you, what would you say?

In Their Shoes

Closing the Year and Moving Forward

Directions: Instructional leaders, coaches, and mentors are not only effective because they bring a wealth of knowledge and experience to their role but also because they connect with their coachees' reality and recall how they felt when they were in the same position.

Since it may have been a few years since you were a first-year teacher, let's take a step back to remember and put ourselves in their shoes.

1. As a first-year teacher, what was the end of your school year like? What emotions did you experience and why?

_____

_____

_____

_____

_____

2. What positive practices did you experience at the end of the year? Knowing what you know now, what experiences would you have recommended?

_____

_____

_____

_____

_____

3. What were your reflections about the progress your students made?

_____

_____

_____

_____

_____

4. What do you wish you had done more of? What do you wish you had done less of?

_____

_____

_____

_____

_____

5. If your present self could go back in time to advise your first-year-teacher self, what advice would you offer?

_____

_____

_____

_____

_____

Coaching Scenario for Leaders

Tamara

Directions: Read the scenario below and consider what you would do if you were Tamara's instructional coach. Then answer the follow-up questions below.

> Tamara returned to the classroom after several years away to care for a family member and returned to teaching this year. She has spent the year aligning her previous experiences with the newer context of schooling. You would like for her to return, as you have witnessed both progress and potential. However, you are not sure what her thoughts are about the future. You see this as an opportunity to re-recruit her.

(Continued)

(Continued)

Follow-Up Questions

1. What question(s) would you pose to Tamara to prompt reflection about the school year?

_____

_____

_____

_____

2. What question(s) would you pose to the teacher to learn about her professional goals?

_____

_____

_____

_____

_____

3. What would be your next steps as her coach?

_____

_____

_____

_____

_____

Leaders Get Clear and Anticipate

With a strong onboarding process, instructional leaders and coaches send a clear message to new teachers about "how we do things." They communicate and reiterate the site's expectations around student engagement. This minimizes ambiguity so new teachers adapt and adopt best practices more quickly than if they were to navigate this theme on their own.

In Our Shoes

Closing the Year and Moving Forward

Directions: Instructional leaders/coaches should pause first to get clear about their expectations. Then they can craft their message and provide onboarded teachers with appropriate feedback to elevate their practice.

1. What are your expectations about the use of instructional time during the final weeks of the year? How is this communicated?

_____

_____

_____

_____

_____

2. Does the site have an end-of-year or inventory list that needs to be completed?

_____

_____

_____

_____

_____

3. What are the guidelines and expectations for end-of-year celebrations with the class?

_____

_____

_____

_____

_____

(Continued)

(Continued)

4. What are the procedures for posting final grades?

_____

_____

_____

_____

_____

5. What are the expectations for teacher involvement in end-of-school-year activities (e.g., Field Day, award assemblies, student performances, graduation)?

_____

_____

_____

_____

_____

Leaders Get Clear and Communicate

Now that you have a clear vision of this cycle's focus and what that looks like at your site, it is important to communicate this message along with your expectations. Below you will find a sample of an onboarding checklist with a suggested timeline for three groups of deliverables: Leader/Coach, New Teacher, and Together.

Onboarding Checklist

	LEADER/COACH	NEW TEACHER	TOGETHER
Week 1	Send a reminder email to new teachers about the final onboarding check-in meeting.	Complete the New Teachers Get Familiar and Implement interactions.	Meet to discuss close-of-school-year procedures and expectations.
	Put a note of appreciation in new teachers' office mailboxes. A handwritten note addressed to the new teacher will light up their day.	Thank the expert teachers who have been involved in your onboarding this year.	

	LEADER/COACH	NEW TEACHER	TOGETHER
	Complete the Context About the Theme section, including the interactions.		
	Complete the Leaders Get Clear and Anticipate section, including the interactions.		
Week 2	Review and reflect on responses from submitted Leaders Ask "How Did We Do?" surveys.		Meet individually with new teachers for a personal check-in. Use the Check-In and Follow-Up Tools for Leaders to guide your discussion.
	Meet as an onboarding team to reflect on the successes of this year's processes. Discuss refinements for next year.		

Email to New Teachers on the First Day of Cycle

(Example)

Hello _____,

These last two weeks of the school year will fly by and I want to make sure that you and I have time to discuss the logistics of closing the school year and to engage in reflective conversation.

We will wrap up the school year with our last onboarding cycle on closing the school year and moving forward. We will schedule two meetings: the first is with your fellow new teachers to discuss procedures for the final weeks. The second will be an individual meeting so that I can learn about your perspectives across the year.

There is a saying that "Through learning you will teach, and in teaching you will learn." I hope both of these have been true for you.

Sincerely,

_____

(Continued)

(Continued)

(Other Conversations to Consider)

- Final district and schoolwide committee meetings
- District summer professional development opportunities
- Local and community events
- End-of-year staff socials and events
- Student events:
  - Theater performances
  - Chorus concerts
  - Band and orchestra concerts
  - Final athletic events, games, and tournaments
  - Promotion and graduation ceremonies

Thank-You Email to Expert Teachers

(Example)

Hello _____,

I want to thank you once again for your professional generosity in opening your classroom to new teachers this year. I have heard many times this year from new teachers about your positive influence on them. Your investment in the next generation of new teachers is evidence of your investment in the future of our school and the profession. I am truly grateful for your willingness to guide.

Please enjoy this 3:45 video from Edutopia, and thank you for remembering what it was like to be a new teacher: "If I Knew Then: A Letter to Me on My First Day of Teaching": https://youtu.be/miPYLJl247g.

Sincerely,

_____

Leaders Express Appreciation

Here is a checklist of ways that leaders/coaches can show a token of their appreciation to new teachers for all of their hard work. This could also show your teachers how to pay it forward. Showing them graciousness will move them to show and connect with their students. We recommend that you do one item from this checklist this month to make them feel welcome and a part of the school.

(Examples)

Write a one- or two-sentence message on a thank-you card. Put it in their office mailbox with a special treat to use during the summer:

- Water bottle

- Sunscreen and a beach towel

- Canvas tote bag with the school logo

- A small plant

- Bookmark for summer reading

- Small paper journal

Expert Tip: Ask parent/family groups, community members, or local businesses for donations.

New Teachers Get Familiar and Implement

Video Reflection

Closing the Year and Moving Forward

Directions: Watch the video of teachers being told by their students why they are the reason these students come to school. Consider your own students and the successes you have had with them this year. After viewing Video 8.1 (available at the companion website), answer the reflective questions below.

1. What student of yours has made the most academic gains this year? What were you able to do to accomplish this?

   _____

   _____

2. Who is your "turnaround" student this year? In other words, who made the most progress socially? What were you able to do to accomplish this?

   _____

   _____

(Continued)

(Continued)

3. Name the student who took big strides this year to drive their learning. What were you able to do to accomplish this?

_____

_____

4. Who is the student you wished you had made more progress with? If you had to do it again, what would you do differently?

_____

_____

5. Consider the four students you named. What advice do you have for their teachers next year?

1.

2.

3.

4.

New Teachers Self-Assess

Reflecting on Teaching and Learning

Directions: Take a moment to assess yourself in these areas.

1. What do you consider to be your biggest accomplishment this year instructionally?

_____

_____

_____

_____

_____

2. What routine or procedure was most frustrating for you? How will you revise this for next year?

_____

_____

_____

_____

3. Where did you struggle the most, instructionally? What do you need to continue to improve in this area?

_____

_____

_____

_____

_____

4. What is a goal you have for yourself in terms of curriculum development next year? What do you need to continue to improve in this area?

_____

_____

_____

_____

_____

5. What is a goal you have for yourself in terms of assessment? What do you need to continue to improve in this area?

_____

_____

_____

_____

_____

Check-In and Follow-Up Tools for Leaders

School leaders are responsible for creating systems to ensure that new teachers continue to grow and effectively deepen their practice. Hold an individual conference with each new teacher to gain insights about their perspectives on the year. The questions in this interview protocol are meant to spark reflective thought, You may have other questions you would like to add.

1. What do you consider to be your greatest success this year? Why?

2. Describe your favorite day of this past school year. What happened?

3. Describe your least favorite day of the school year. What happened?

4. What student improved most this year? Why do you think they were successful?

5. What was a major challenge you faced this year?

6. What helped you to be able to address those challenges?

7. How do you believe your students would describe you?

8. Who influenced your professional practice most this year?

9. How was your communication with families?

10. If you could advise beginning-of-the-school-year you, what would you say?

Leaders Cycle Back With New Teachers

Thank you for your tireless commitment to our students! As we move forward through our progressions, it is important to revisit what we learned previously so we don't forget and continue to grow in those areas.

Directions: Reflect on a previous theme of your choice and answer the questions below.

Previous Theme(s)

- Setting up the physical classroom, routines, and procedures
- Student engagement and universal classroom management
- Teacher credibility, teacher expectations, and family communications
- Teacher clarity (learning intentions, relevance, and success criteria)
- Fostering student ownership of learning and using evidence-based instructional practices
- Formative assessment and feedback
- Summative assessments and grading

1. What new takeaways or aha moments did you encounter? What new understandings have you reached this month about the theme you selected?

2. In what ways have you continued to develop professionally in this area?

3. What lingering questions or wonderings do you have for a leader, coach, or expert teacher?

4. What will you be sure to do in the next school year, as it relates to the theme you selected?

Leaders Ask "How Did We Do?"

Moving Forward
It is very important for me to gauge my effectiveness as a coach because I want to provide a professional environment that invests in your growth. Please help me in meeting this goal.
Reflect on your experiences this year with the onboarding process.
Using the following scale, with 1 being not confident, 3 being somewhat confident, and 5 indicating very confident, how confident are you in your preparation and readiness for the next school year?

"I know where I'm going." I understand my current performance and how it relates to my professional growth.	 Please elaborate:
"I have the tools for the journey." I understand that I can select from a range of strategies to move my learning forward, especially when progress is interrupted.	 Please elaborate:
"I monitor my progress." I seek and respond to feedback from others to assess my own performance. I know that making mistakes is expected and indicates an opportunity for further learning.	 Please elaborate:
"I recognize when I'm ready for what's next." I make my own observations to identify when I'm ready to move on.	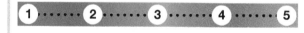 Please elaborate:

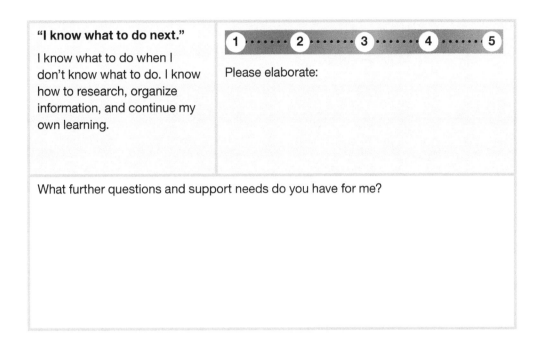

"I know what to do next."

I know what to do when I don't know what to do. I know how to research, organize information, and continue my own learning.

1 ...... 2 ...... 3 ...... 4 5

Please elaborate:

What further questions and support needs do you have for me?

Tying It Together With Trust

Recall the five facets of trustworthiness in leaders (benevolence, reliability, competence, honesty, and openness) from page 34. Consider taking a moment to pause and reflect on your behaviors and interactions with your staff in the final weeks of the school year:

▶ In what ways did you develop trust specifically with new teachers?

▶ Were there any instances in which you unintentionally acted in a way that might have resulted in lowering their trust?

▶ As we move into the next school year, what will you continue doing? What will you start doing? What will you stop doing?

Trust Recalibration

Looking Back to Move Forward

	EVIDENCE OF TRUSTING BEHAVIORS	EVIDENCE OF DISTRUSTING BEHAVIORS	HOW WILL I MAINTAIN OR DEVELOP TRUST NEXT SCHOOL YEAR?
(1) Benevolence			
(2) Reliability			
(3) Competence			
(4) Honesty			
(5) Openness			

Conclusion

Tying the knot on an entire school year can be quite daunting! There are things that you wish you had done differently. Use these insights to strengthen next year's plans. This playbook focused on onboarding new teachers, with an aim of providing practical ways to make connections and grow in meaningful ways. Each year you will continue to make strides in different areas, and our hope is that you developed new and strategic ways to create and use these tools. The pages of the playbook are a place to capture your creativity and new insights. We hope that you wrote down new ways to make connections and provide meaningful reflection for growth. Your path will continue to inspire and help others to be their best.

Additional Resources

For Leaders and Coaches

Lassiter, C., Fisher, D., Frey, N., & Smith, D. (2022). *How leadership works: A playbook for instructional leaders.* Corwin.

A 5-Minute Read for New Teachers

York-Barr, J., & Ghere, G. (2017, July 10). Reflective practice: An educator's pathway to learn from and continuously improve teaching. *Corwin Connect.* https://corwin-connect.com/2017/07/reflective-practice-educators-pathway-learn-continuously-improve-teaching-practice/

A 5-Minute Read for Expert Teachers

Aguilar, E. (2013). Transformation begins with reflection: How was your year? *Edutopia.* https://www.edutopia.org/blog/transformation-begins-with-reflection-elena-aguilar

Visit the companion website at
https://qrs.ly/9mesfwe
for additional resources.

References

Aguilar, E. (2013). Transformation begins with reflection: How was your year? *Edutopia*. https://www.edutopia.org/blog/transformation-begins-with-reflection-elena-aguilar

Almarode, J., Fisher, D., & Frey, N. (2021). *How learning works: A playbook*. Corwin.

Almarode, J., Fisher, D., & Frey, N. (2022). *How feedback works: A playbook*. Corwin.

Angelo, T. A., & Cross, K. P. (1993). *Classroom assessment techniques: A handbook for college teachers* (2nd ed.). John Wiley & Sons.

Berry, A. (2022). *Reimagining student engagement: From disrupting to driving*. Corwin.

Burke, P. F., Aubusson, P. J., Schuck, S. R., Buchanan, J. D., & Prescott, A. E. (2015). How do early career teachers value different types of support? A scale-adjusted latent class choice model. *Teaching and Teacher Education, 47*, 241–253.

Corwin. (n.d.). Professional learning services built for impact on all learners. *Corwin*. https://us.corwin.com/en-us/nam/visible-learning

Corwin. (2021a, April 26). The game of grading with Tom Guskey: Corwin leaders coaching leaders podcast. *Corwin YouTube Channel*. https://youtu.be/uoDKzYaQQEo

Corwin. (2021b, September 14). John Almarode and Nancy Frey: A look at how learning works. *Corwin YouTube Channel*. https://youtu.be/GouaXTmCZXk

Costa, A. L., & Garmston, R. J. (2015). *Cognitive coaching: Developing self-directed leaders and learners* (3rd ed.). Rowman & Littlefield.

Crichton, H., & McDaid, A. (2016). Learning intentions and success criteria: Learners' and teachers' views. *Curriculum Journal, 27*(2), 190–203.

Donohoo, J., Bryen, S., & Weishar, B. (2019, June 27). A matrix of feedback for learning: A brief summary. *Corwin Connect*. https://corwin-connect.com/2019/06/a-matrix-of-feedback-for-learning-a-brief-summary/?fbclid=IwAR13WxLMZ93_tZeasNopfFTCHw1crPb23k96lbG6BI31MwLyLiS-CrfPcSMU

Doyle, L., Easterbrook, M. J., & Harris, P. R. (2023). Roles of socioeconomic status, ethnicity and teacher beliefs in academic grading. *British Journal of Educational Psychology, 93*(1), 91–112.

Education Hub. (n.d.). *High impact teaching: How to develop high expectations teaching*. https://theeducationhub.org.nz/wp-content/uploads/2018/06/How-to-develop-high-expectations-teaching.pdf

Edutopia. (2014, May 3). If I knew then: A letter to me on my first day teaching. *Edutopia YouTube Channel*. https://youtu.be/miPYLJI247g

Epstein, J. L., Sanders, M. G., Sheldon, S. B., Simon, B. S., Salinas, K. C., Jansorn, N. R., Voorhis, F. L. V., Martin, C. S., Thomas, B. G., Greenfeld, M. D., Hutchins, D. J., & Williams, K. J. (2019). *School, family, and community partnerships: Your handbook for action*. Corwin.

Fantuzzo, J., McWayne, C., Perry, M. A., & Childs, S. (2004). Multiple dimensions of family involvement and their relations to behavioral and learning competencies for urban, low-income children. *School Psychology Review, 33*(4), 467–480.

Feldman, J. C. (2018). *Grading for equity: What it is, why it matters, and how it can transform schools and classrooms*. Corwin.

Fendick, F. (1990). *The correlation between teacher clarity of communication and student achievement gain: A meta-analysis* [Unpublished doctoral dissertation]. University of Florida, Gainesville.

Fisher, D., & Frey, N. (2020, June 5). 5 tips for increasing clarity in the mathematics classroom. *Corwin Connect*. https://corwin-connect.com/2020/06/5-tips-for-increasing-clarity-in-the-mathematics-classroom/?utm_source=rss&utm_medium=rss&utm_campaign=5-tips-for-increasing-clarity-in-the-mathematics-classroom

Fisher, D., & Frey, N. (2021a). *Better learning through structured teaching* (3rd ed.). ASCD.

Fisher, D., & Frey, N. (2021b, November 9). How to implement learning intentions and success criteria in the classroom. *Fisher and Frey YouTube Channel*. https://youtu.be/xqBdPjSE--g

Fisher, D., Frey, N., Almarode, J., Flories, K., & Nagel, D. (2019). *The PLC+ playbook: A hands-on guide to collectively improving student learning*. Corwin.

Fisher, D., Frey, N., Amador, O., & Assof, J. (2018). *The teacher clarity playbook, grades K-12*. Corwin.

Fisher, D., Frey, N., & Hattie, J. (2016). *Visible learning for literacy: Implementing the practices that work best to accelerate student learning*. Corwin.

Fisher, D., Frey, N., Hattie, J., & Ortega, S. (2023). *Teaching students to drive their learning*. Corwin.

Fisher, D., Frey, N., Lassiter, C., & Smith, D. (2022). *Leader credibility: The essential traits of those who engage, inspire, and transform*. Corwin.

Fisher, D., Frey, N., Ortega, S., & Hattie, J. (2023). *Teaching students to drive their learning: A playbook on engagement and self-regulation, K–12*. Corwin.

Fisher, D., Frey, N., Quaglia, R. J., Smith, D., & Lande, L. L. (2018). *Engagement by design: Creating learning environments where students thrive*. Corwin.

Frahm, M., & Cianca, M. (2021). Will they stay or will they go? Leadership behaviors that increase teacher retention in rural schools. *The Rural Educator, 42*(3), 1–13.

Frey, N., & Fisher, D. (2010). Identifying instructional moves during guided instruction. *The Reading Teacher, 64*(2), 84–95.

Gallup. (2019). *Gallup's perspective on creating an exceptional onboarding process for new employees*. https://www.gallup.com/workplace/247076/onboarding-new-employees-perspective-paper.aspx?thank-you-report-form=1

Gonsor, S. (2022, July 29). The qualities of exceptional mentor teachers. *Edutopia*. https://www.edutopia.org/article/qualities-exceptional-mentor-teachers/

Gordon, B. (2018, March 23). A five-word answer to student engagement. *Corwin Connect*. https://corwin-connect.com/2018/03/the-five-word-answer-to-student-engagement/

Greenstein, L. (2019, February 19). *Overcoming assessment bias: Making assessment fair for all learners*. https://www.assessmentnetwork.net/2019/02/overcomingassessment-bias-making-assessment-fair-for-all-learners

Griffin, R., & Townsley, M. (2022). Including homework and employability skills in class grades: An investigation of equitable grading outcomes in an urban high school. *Practical Assessment, Research & Evaluation, 27*, 1–12.

Guskey, T. R. (2011). Five obstacles to grading reform. *Educational Leadership, 69*(3), 16–21.

Hargraves, V. (2018). High expectations self-assessment checklist: How to develop high expectation teaching. *The Education Hub*. https://theeducationhub.org.nz/how-to-develop-high-expectations-teaching

Hattie, J. (2023). *Visible learning: The sequel: A synthesis of over 2100 meta-analyses relating to achievement*. Routledge.

Hattie, J., & Zierer, K. (2018). *10 mindframes for visible learning: Teaching for success*. Routledge.

Hine, M. G. (2022). Words matter: Differences in informative and negative school communication in engaging families. *School Community Journal, 32*(1), 157–185.

Hylton, S. P., & Colley, A. C. (2022). For small districts, a regional network holds the key to new teacher support. *Learning Professional, 43*(4), 52–56.

Jackson, P. W. (1968). *Life in classrooms*. Holt, Rinehart and Winston.

Kagan, L., Kagan, M., & Kagan, S. (1997). *Cooperative learning structures for teambuilding*. Kagan Publishing.

Klassen, R. M., & Chiu, M. M. (2010). Effects on teachers' self-efficacy and job satisfaction: Teacher gender years of experience, and job stress. *Journal of Educational Psychology, 102*(3), 741–756.

König, J., Santagata, R., Scheiner, T., Adleff, A.-K., Yang, X., & Kaiser, G. (2022). Teacher noticing: A systematic literature review of conceptualizations, research designs, and findings on learning to notice. *Educational Research Review, 36*, 100453. https://doi.org/10.1016/j.edurev.2022.100453

Kreisberg, H. (2022, January 11). 3 tips to enhance communication with families. *Corwin Connect*. https://corwin-connect.com/2022/01/3-tips-to-enhance-communication-with-families-about-their-childs-math-before-years-end/

Lassiter, C., Fisher, D., Frey, N., & Smith, D. (2022). *How leadership works: A playbook for instructional leaders*. Corwin.

Martin, N. K., Schafer, N. J., McClowry, S., Emmer, E. T., Brekelmans, M., Mainhard, T., & Wubbels, T. (2016). Expanding the definition of classroom management: Recurring themes and new conceptualizations. *Journal of Classroom Interactions, 51*, 36–45.

McTighe, J. (2021, January 28). 8 quick checks for understanding. *Edutopia*. https://www.edutopia.org/article/8-quick-checks-understanding/

Miller, R. L., King, J. A., Mark, M. M., & Caracelli, V. (2016). The oral history of evaluation: The professional development of Robert Stake. *American Journal of Evaluation, 37*(2), 287–294.

Mosby, A., & Hamilton, S. (2022, September 14). The role of cognition in the gradual release of responsibility model. *Edutopia*. https://www.edutopia.org/article/role-cognition-gradual-release-responsibility-model/

Murdock-Perriera, L. A., & Sedlacek, Q. C. (2018). Questioning Pygmalion in the twenty-first century:

The formation, transmission, and attributional influence of teacher expectancies. *Social Psychology of Education, 21*(3), 691–707.

Napper, K. (2019, June 26). The necessity of having high expectations. *Edutopia.* https://www.edutopia.org/article/necessity-having-high-expectations/

Pariser, S. (2018, September 6). Prep where it counts before the start of school. *Corwin Connect.* https://corwin-connect.com/2018/09/prep-where-it-counts-before-the-start-of-school/

Protheroe, N. (2006). The principal's role in supporting new teachers. *Principal, 86*(2), 34–38.

Purkey, W. W., & Novak, J. M. (1996). *Inviting school success: A self-concept approach to teaching, learning, and democratic practice* (3rd ed.). Wadsworth Publishing.

Quaglia Institute. (2019). *Student voice: A decade of data in grades 6-12.* Author. https://quaglia institute.org/uploads/legacy/Student_Voice_Grades_6-12_Decade_of_Data_Report.pdf

Quinn, D. M. (2020). Experimental evidence on teachers' racial bias in student evaluation: The role of grading scales. *Educational Evaluation and Policy Analysis, 42*(3), 375–392. https://doi.org/10.3102/0162373720932188

Radford, C. P. (2017). *The first years matter: Becoming an effective teacher.* Corwin.

Rogers, A. P., Reagan, E. M., & Ward, C. (2022). Preservice teacher performance assessment and novice teacher assessment literacy. *Teaching Education, 33*(2), 175–193.

Rubie-Davies, C. (2014). *Becoming a high expectation teacher: Raising the bar.* Routledge.

Rubie-Davies, C. M. (2007). Classroom interactions: Exploring the practices of high and low expectation teachers. *British Journal of Educational Psychology, 77*, 289–306.

School Reform Initiative. (2023). *Protocols.* https://www.schoolreforminitiative.org/protocols/

Smith, D., Fisher, D., & Frey, N. (2022). *The restorative practices playbook: Tools for transforming discipline in schools.* Corwin.

Sweeney, D., Harris, L. S., & Steele, J. (2022). *Moves for launching a new year of student-centered coaching.* Corwin.

Terada, Y. (2023, March 17). Why the 100-point grading scale is a stacked deck. *Edutopia.* https://www.edutopia.org/article/why-the-100-point-grading-scale-is-a-stacked-deck

Tschannen-Moran, M. (2004). *Trust matters: Leadership for successful schools.* Jossey-Bass.

Tschannen-Moran, M., & Gareis, C. R. (2015). Principals, trust and vibrant schools. *Societies, 5*(2), 256–276. https://doi.org/10.3390/soc5020256

Tversky, A., & Kahneman, D. (1974). Judgment under uncertainty: Heuristics and biases. *Science, 185*(4157), 1124–1131.

Vasquez, J. (1989). Contexts of learning for minority students. *The Education Forum, 52*(3), 243–253.

Visible Learning Meta^X. (2021). https://www.visible learningmetax.com

Weinberg, A. (2021, July 19). 3 strategies for productive teacher mentoring. *Edutopia.* https://www.edutopia.org/article/3-strategies-productive-teacher-mentoring/

Wlodkowski, R. J. (1983). *Motivational opportunities for successful teaching* [Leader's guide]. Universal Dimensions.

York-Barr, J., & Ghere, G. (2017, July 10). Reflective practice: An educator's pathway to learn from and continuously improve teaching. *Corwin Connect.* https://corwin-connect.com/2017/07/reflective-practice-educators-pathway-learn-continuously-improve-teaching-practice/

Zhang, S., Nishimoto, M., & Liu K. (2019). Preservice teacher expectations of the principal's role in teacher induction. *New Waves Educational Research and Development, 22*(1), 72–89.

Index

A Sage Company

Helping educators make the greatest impact

CORWIN HAS ONE MISSION: to enhance education through intentional professional learning.

We build long-term relationships with our authors, educators, clients, and associations who partner with us to develop and continuously improve the best evidence-based practices that establish and support lifelong learning.

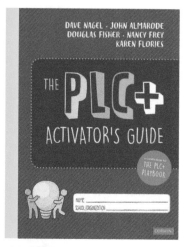

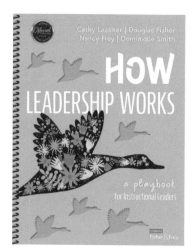

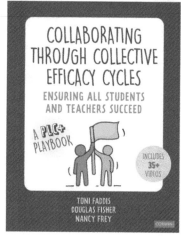
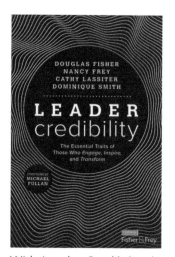

When you're ready to take your learning deeper, begin your journey with our PD services. Our personalized professional learning workshops are designed for schools or districts who want to engage in high-quality PD with a certified consultant, measure their progress, and evaluate their impact on student learning.

CORWIN PLC+

Empower teacher teams to build collective agency and remove learning barriers

It's not enough to just build teacher agency, we must also focus on the power of the collective. Empowering your PLCs is a step toward becoming better equipped educators with greater credibility to foster successful learners.

Get started at corwin.com/plc

CORWIN Teacher Clarity

Students learn more when expectations are clear

As both a method and a mindset, Teacher Clarity allows the classroom to transform into a place where teaching is made clear. Learn how to explicitly communicate to students what they will be learning on a given day, why they're learning it, and how to know if they were successful.

Get started at corwin.com/teacherclarity

CORWIN Visible Learning+®

Translate the science of how we learn into practices for the classroom

Discover how learning works and how this translates into potential for enhancing and accelerating learning. Learn how to develop a shared language of learning and implement the science of learning in schools and classrooms.

Get started at corwin.com/visiblelearning